Eduard Lohse

The author: Eduard Lohse, Professor of New Testament Theology at the University of Göttingen in Germany and contributor to Kittel's *Theological Dictionary of the N.T.*, has lectured widely in the United States.

The translator: Martin O. Dietrich, Professor of German at Earlham College, is the translator of *A Life of Luther*, by Oskar Thulin, a Fortress Press publication.

History of the
Suffering and
Death of
Jesus Christ

History of the Suffering and Death of Jesus Christ

by EDUARD LOHSE

translated by MARTIN O. DIETRICH

FORTRESS PRESS, PHILADELPHIA

3671J66   Printed in U.S.A.   UB86

Preface

This book grew out of a series of lectures originally delivered in the spring of 1962 at the Kirchliche Hochschule in
Berlin and again one year later at various theological seminaries in the United States. The lectures have been reworked
and expanded prior to publication. I should like to express
my thanks to the Lutheran World Federation for the pleasure and privilege accorded me of visiting the United States
and lecturing at a number of Lutheran seminaries. I remember with gratitude the hospitality shown me by the various
faculties and student bodies, and particularly the interest they
showed in the lectures. In the ensuing discussions our common endeavor was to gain fresh perspectives on the familiar
biblical narratives. The fruits of these conversations have
been gratefully taken into account in the final formulation
of the text. To the translator of the book, Doctor Martin O.
Dietrich, I should like to express my sincere appreciation for
the care and precision with which he has worked.

Göttingen   Eduard Lohse
May, 1966

Contents

1. The Earliest Account of Jesus' Passion 1

2. Jesus' Entry into Jerusalem and the
   Cleansing of the Temple 20

3. The Institution of the Lord's Supper 35

4. Gethsemane 55

5. The Trial 69

6. The Crucifixion 89

Indexes 105

1.

The Earliest Account
of Jesus' Passion

The evangelist Mark, who was the first to give a written account of the life, suffering, and death of Jesus of Nazareth, specifies at the very outset the cause which his book is intended to serve—the words stand almost like a title at the beginning of his presentation—"the gospel of Jesus Christ" (Mark 1:1). The evangelist thus adopts an expression which in the earliest Christian proclamation had already assumed a fixed form and content. For the joyous message which was heralded to all the world by the first Christians had but a single burden—the declaration of Jesus Christ, the proclamation of him as Lord, and the invitation to all who heard the preaching to believe in him.

That this is the substance of the gospel is indicated also by the Apostle Paul when in the first verses of his Letter to the Romans he says that he was called to be an apostle and was set apart for "the gospel of God which he promised beforehand through his prophets in the holy scriptures," namely —and here is where he pinpoints the heart of the matter— "the gospel concerning his Son, who was descended from David according to the flesh and designated Son of God in power according to the Spirit of holiness by his resurrection from the dead, Jesus Christ our Lord" (Rom. 1:1-4). In these verses Paul makes use of an established formula employed by the early Christian churches to express in succinct form their confession of faith. The one gospel, besides which there can be no other (cf. Gal. 1:6-9), has as its content the suffering, death, and resurrection of Jesus Christ, his humiliation and exaltation; it proclaims him as the Messiah and Lord.

The evangelist's purpose, therefore, is to share in this task common to all Christians. His written account is intended as a contribution to the cause of proclaiming Christ. He writes, not as a reporter determined to record in detail the sequence of certain events, but in order to pass on the message concerning Jesus Christ in such a way as to summon his readers to an acceptance of the gospel, or to strengthen and confirm in faith those who already believe. "These are written that you may believe that Jesus is the Christ, the Son of God, and that believing you may have life in his name," writes the fourth evangelist at the end of his book (John 20:31). Mark might very well have described his own objective in similar fashion.

For several decades all that was known of Jesus had been passed down by word of mouth. His preaching, his disputes with spokesmen for the various Jewish groups, the signs and deeds he performed, and above all the path of suffering which led him to the cross were talked about, preached on at the worship services, and recounted in the periods of instruction. In no case was this activity of Jesus thought of as belongingly solely to the past. To be sure, Jesus had made his appearance at a very specific moment in history, his whole life was lived out within the confines of the Jewish lands whose borders he never traversed, and he met his end on a cross outside the gates of Jerusalem. His followers, however, proclaim him as the Christ who was raised from death and exalted unto God, who now reigns as Lord and whom his church presently confesses. What this means is that the Christ-event could and can be proclaimed only in such a way as to express clearly its present validity. That is why it was impossible simply to offer a report dealing with bygone events. Speech about Christ had to take the form of confession and proclamation, in which the living voice of the gospel is heard here and now.

The fact that among the earliest Christians speech about

Christ was of this character explains why the traditions concerning Jesus' words and deeds, his life and passion, were
decisively shaped and stamped by the witness of the church.
The so-called "form-critical" investigation of the Gospels,
begun four decades ago with the pioneering efforts of Karl
Ludwig Schmidt, Martin Dibelius, and Rudolf Bultmann,[1] is
mainly an effort to discover the shape of the oral tradition
which preceded the written accounts. Its purpose is by no
means merely to categorize the various types of narratives and
traditions according to their literary form. Its aim is rather
to trace the influence which the problems and purposes
of the earliest Christians had in determining the shape or
form of the tradition prior to the time when the orally transmitted materials were finally recorded in our Gospels. Form-
critical investigation endeavors to lay bare the oldest stratum
of the tradition about Jesus and to interpret the texts of the
Gospels in the light of their own specific and characteristic
principles. In this connection it is essential to note carefully
what each particular text is all about, for the church will
have treated the transmitted materials differently according
as they had to do with the words of Jesus, the miracle stories,
or his *via dolorosa*. In every interpretation of the Gospels,
therefore, it is necessary to keep constantly in mind the
question concerning the way in which the confession and
proclamation of the Christian church has shaped the account
of the story of Jesus.

Even a cursory glance at their general outline discloses the
fact that within the Gospels the story of the passion unquestionably constitutes the most important part. In terms of
bulk alone the account of Jesus' last days in Jerusalem, his
suffering and death, represents a strikingly large part of the
whole—five full chapters in the case of Mark (11-15). It is

---

1 Karl Ludwig Schmidt, *Der Rahmen der Geschichte Jesu* (Berlin, 1919);
Martin Dibelius, *Die Formgeschichte des Evangeliums* (Tübingen, 1919; 3d
ed. 1959), trans. Bertram Lee Woolf as *From Tradition to Gospel* (New
York: Scribner, 1935) Rudolf Bultmann, *Die Geschichte der synoptischen
Tradition* (Göttingen, 1921; 3d ed., 1957); trans. John Marsh as *The History
of the Synoptic Tradition* (Oxford: Blackwell, 1963).

furthermore noteworthy that in respect to the passion story
the accounts of the Four Gospels are in closer agreement than
in respect to any other portion of their contents. This leads us
to the conclusion that already at a very early date there must
have existed an account of Jesus' suffering which mentioned
the various episodes of the passion journey and described
what took place in each. This account, passed along by word
of mouth within the Christian churches, constitutes the
foundation on which the four evangelists build. What then
do we know about this oldest form of the passion story, this
account which the earliest Christians gave concerning the
suffering of their Lord?

The earliest written statement of the matter is that of the
Apostle Paul at the beginning of the fifteenth chapter of his
First Letter to the Corinthians. What Paul here asserts, and
with express assurance underscores, is the fact that he once
brought the gospel to the Corinthians and delivered it to
them even as he had himself received it. He emphasizes
particularly the fact that he transmitted the message about
Christ in the shape of a fixed formulation—a *logos*—and
that the Corinthians had received this message. It is the same
glad message that all the apostles and missionaries were proclaiming, which in substance is this: "that Christ died for
our sins in accordance with the scriptures, that he was
buried, that he was raised on the third day in accordance
with the scriptures, and that he appeared to Cephas, then to
the twelve" (I Cor. 15:3-5). The very way in which Paul
introduces this statement calls attention to the fact that what
he is about to say is a quotation. Following this introduction
comes the quotation itself, dealing with the death and rising
of Christ and referring to the appearances of the risen Lord
to Cephas and the twelve. The text itself shows clearly that
the quotation extends only to this point, concluding with
the last word of verse 5. For up to this point Paul is citing
the transmitted phraseology of the earliest Christian kerygma
in the form of subordinate clauses. The two longer phrases
(died—raised) are each accompanied by a shorter subordi-

nate clause (buried—appeared). A new start, however, is made with verse 6, for now there begins a series of main clauses which speak of further appearances of the risen One.

It is not only the apostle's introduction but more particularly the linguistic form of the phrases themselves which shows that the statement taken over by Paul and quoted in verses 3-5 must have had its origin in the primitive Palestinian church. For this statement contains a number of expressions not used elsewhere by Paul. This is the only passage in all the Pauline letters, for example, that mentions the circle of "the twelve." Elsewhere Paul speaks always of "the apostles." When referring to the Old Testament, Paul never makes use of the expression here used twice: "in accordance with the scriptures." Instead he always says, "as it is written," or a similar expression. In his own writing the apostle rarely employs the plural when speaking of sin, as was customarily done among the Jews and also among the earliest Christians who had in mind the multiplicity of sinful acts. Paul almost always uses the singular, having in mind instead the cosmic power to which the race of Adam is enslaved. These observations lead us to conclude that these phrases were not formulated by Paul himself. He simply took them over and was now passing them on to others.

Beyond all this, Joachim Jeremias has convincingly shown that though these sentences were indeed written in Greek, there is no doubt that linguistically they go back to a Semitic original.[2] Their Semitic character can be seen already in the strictly parallel structure of the paired clauses: died . . . buried, raised . . . appeared. In both cases a specific reference is made to "the scriptures," the plural form reflecting the ancient Hebrew way of referring to the sacred writings. Then too the passive form "he was raised" replaces the active "God raised him." In Judaism it was customary to guard against any possible misuse of the divine name by avoiding the use of it altogether and substituting instead a circum-

[2] See Joachim Jeremias, *The Eucharistic Words of Jesus*, trans. Norman Perrin (London: SCM Press, 1966), pp. 101-103.

locution. The statement in question, for example, gets around it by using the passive voice. The fact that the word for "being seen" has here the significance of "he appeared" can likewise be traced back to a Semitic expression in which the passive of the verb "to see" can mean either "he was seen" or "he appeared."

It can no longer be determined with certainty whether the phrases in I Corinthians 15:3-5 were originally formulated in Aramaic—as Jeremias surmises—or in Hebrew. Since the discovery at Qumran, on the banks of the Dead Sea, of a large number of Hebrew manuscripts deriving from the period just prior to the New Testament, it will again be necessary to reckon more strongly with the possibility that in Palestine all affirmations involving doctrine, faith, or confession were composed in the language of the Scriptures, that is, in Hebrew. At this point, of course, we cannot go into these philological questions in any detail. For our purposes it will suffice simply to indicate the results of our analysis of the verses under consideration. What the early church in Jerusalem was saying in these brief affirmations of its common confession is that the suffering of the Messiah was for our sins and in accordance with the Scriptures. What does it really mean, though, to speak in this way about the death of the Christ?

The first thing to note is that the earliest Christian confession of faith names the cross and resurrection of Jesus as the one event on which our salvation is based. His death and resurrection are properly understood only in terms of their indissoluble interconnection, their close mutual interrelationship. For it is only because Christ was raised from death that his dying is imbued with atoning power and men's sins are forgiven (cf. I Cor. 15:17). Apart from Easter, Good Friday would mean only death, not victory over death. At the same time, however, the earliest Christian confession stresses the fact that the risen and exalted Lord is identical with the historical Jesus who died on the cross for us. The Christian church, therefore, in reporting the suffering of Jesus, does not speak merely of an event of the past, one that happened some time ago and no longer has any direct connection with the present. On the contrary, the church heralds this event precisely because the very Jesus who is being proclaimed now, today, as the Lord is the same Jesus who trod the path to Calvary.

That the Messiah should end his life on a cross in misery and suffering, that he should meet his death flanked by two criminals, as an outcast from the holy city—these things, to be sure, stood in sharp contradiction to the expectations which the Jews of that day attached to the Messiah. Recently discovered manuscripts have enabled us to see more clearly than ever how diverse and varied were the current conceptions of the Messiah's advent. While the Pharisees, and the Jewish people generally, were hoping the anointed king would appear as a second David and restore the glory of Israel, there were others who were looking instead for a prophet like Moses, or a high priest of the last days who would purify Israel and prepare it for God's new world. Of an entirely different sort was the apocalyptically conceived picture according to which men's eyes were directed toward the heavens from whence the Son of man was to descend on the clouds to judge the godless and set at liberty the righteous. For all their differences, however, these conceptions of the Messiah and of the day of salvation agreed in this: God's anointed was to come forth as the ruler and judge who would put an end to the lowliness of Israel, drive out the heathen, and establish the kingdom of glory.

Nowhere is there any reference to a suffering Messiah who would take upon himself the burden of humiliation and death for the sins of the people. The question has of course been raised whether in the smaller Jewish communities there might possibly have existed the conception of a suffering Messiah.[3] But is highly improbable that this notion could

---

[3] See Joachim Jeremias, "Pais Theou," in Gerhard Kittel (ed.), *Theologisches Wörterbuch zum Neuen Testament*, (Stuttgart, 1933–   ), 680ff.; published in English translation in W. Zimmerli and J. Jeremias, *The Servant of God* (London: SCM, 1957), pp. 43 ff.

have existed anywhere in pre-Christian Judaism. For wherever the relationship of man to God is based solely on the law, wherever righteousness by law is the fundamental consideration and no way of salvation is known except that of the divine law, there no room can remain for a suffering Messiah who takes upon himself the guilt of others. We can readily understand, therefore, how shocking it must have been for the Jews to hear it said that the Christ—which after all means the Messiah—died for our sins.

"For our sins"—the words express the fact that it was our sins, the separation from God brought about by our guilt, which made it necessary for the Messiah to suffer and to die. He stepped into the breach which we were not able to close. He did this, however, in order to remove our sins from us, so that we might become free. On a later occasion Paul expresses the same idea in his own terminology: "For our sake he made him to be sin who knew no sin, so that in him we might become the righteousness of God" (II Cor. 5:21). The Messiah suffered and died that we might receive the forgiveness of sins. The fact that he drank the cup of suffering right down to the very dregs is underscored by the mention of the grave: ". . . that he was buried." Thus he died our death and was laid in a grave, even as we must all die and be buried.

But how could this be, that the Messiah instead of appearing in glory and majesty should offer up his life on the accursed tree? From the very beginning Christian preaching has always answered this question by saying that this was God's will—it pleased God to have it so.

It has adduced as evidence for this answer the testimony of Scripture: "The Messiah died for our sins—in accordance with the scriptures." In this appeal to "the scriptures" what was doubtless intended was primarily a reference to those passages which deal with the suffering and death of the righteous One, who has to endure misery and persecution at the hands of the wicked. Christians repeatedly connected Psalms 22, 31, and 69 with the account of Jesus' passion. The clearest reference, however, was to the suffering of God's Servant in the fifty-third chapter of the Book of Isaiah: "he has borne our griefs" (vs. 4) ; "he was wounded for our transgressions" (vs. 5) ; "they made his grave with the wicked" (vs. 9) ; "he shall bear their iniquities" (vs. 11) ; "he poured out his soul to death, and . . . bore the sin of many" (vs. 12).

When in the earliest Christian kerygma reference is made to "the scriptures," however, the intention is not simply to single out individual verses of the Old Testament but to express something far more basic. All of Scripture is construed to be a witness to and about Christ, and hence is claimed for and by the Christian church. And conversely, the real meaning of the Scriptures formerly hidden, can be understood only from the vantage point of the Christ-event. This understanding of the Old Testament represented a polemical departure from that which had been developed within the synagogue, whereby the law was taken to be the heart and core of the Scriptures. The key to a proper understanding of what is written is not the law but the message about Christ. The New Testament reference to the authority of Holy Scripture confronted the Jews with the claim that those Old Testament passages dealing with the suffering and death of God's Servant are not fully comprehended apart from the Christian understanding of the Messiah. Thus "the scriptures" are mentioned to show that the suffering, death, and resurrection of the Messiah has its basis in the plan and decree of God. The reference to the Scriptures represents in addition a defense of the Christian message against Jewish objections and at the same time an effort to win over Jewish hearers to the point where they will affirm and accept the gospel.

This is why the early Christians could hardly speak of the suffering and death of Jesus without employing the language of the Old Testament. In the various episodes of the passion story Old Testament quotations and expressions are to be found at every point, not just where a scriptural quotation is expressly prefaced by a specific introduction but even more frequently as an integral part of the continuing narrative.[4] And it is not merely a case of certain events in the *via dolorosa* being described in terms of Old Testament imagery, events such as the mockery of Jesus, his crucifixion between two malefactors, and his burial. On the contrary, there is no doubt but that study of the Old Testament also led to the inclusion in the passion story of individual sayings from the Psalms and the prophets in such a way that they helped to shape the narrative.

Frequently we can no longer determine with any assurance whether particular statements and expressions in the passion story are intended to recount actual happenings or whether they have simply been taken over as a part of the proof from Scripture and then used to embellish the narrative. Thus, for example, the statement that a drink of vinegar is offered to the crucified One (Mark 15:23, 36; Matt. 27:34, 48; Luke 23:36; John 19:29) agrees perfectly with Psalm 69:21. That lots are cast for the garments of the innocent victim (Mark 15:24; Luke 23:34; John 19:24) is mentioned already in Psalm 22:18. The words that the dying Jesus utters on the cross (Mark 15:34) are from the Old Testament: "My God, my God, why hast thou forsaken me?" (Ps. 22:1). It is true that this cry points up the anguish of desolation which has seized the praying One in the depths of his suffering; but this very distress is expressed in a word from the Scriptures in which Jesus calls upon God and addresses him as "my God." In saying that Jesus spoke this word, the evangelists would again call attention to the connection with Scripture: it was by God's will and pleasure that his servant, the anointed One, had to suffer and die.

It was our examination of the phraseology of the earliest kerygma which led to this brief consideration of the passion story as told by the evangelists. But now we must return to the question with which we began: Of what did the earliest account of Jesus' passion consist? I Corinthians 15:3-5 cites

4 See Dibelius, *From Tradition to Gospel, op. cit.,* pp. 186 ff.; and Bultmann, *The History of the Synoptic Tradition, op. cit.,* pp. 280 ff.

certain affirmations from the earliest Christian proclamation which make mention only in brief and summary fashion of the fact that Jesus Christ suffered and died, and of the significance of that fact. But since the fact of Christ's passion is of such fundamental significance for the church's faith and preaching, not only was the event of the crucifixion mentioned as the subject of that faith and confession but the whole story of how this event took place was also recounted, the story of the entire passion and the course it followed. We can determine with some precision what these orally transmitted reports may have been like by examining the terminology of certain passages in the Gospels.

Mark reports on three different occasions that Jesus solemnly announced to his disciples that the Son of man would have to suffer, die, and rise again (Mark 8:31; 9:31; 10:33-34). Matthew and Luke took over from Mark this tradition of Jesus' speaking of the matter three times (Matt. 16:21; 17:22-23; 20:17-19; Luke 9:22, 44; 18:31-33). Since they base their accounts upon Mark, we can start with the Marcan version under the assumption that it is the earliest of the three. In Mark 10:33-34 we read: "Behold, we are going up to Jerusalem; and the Son of man will be delivered to the chief priests and the scribes, and they will condemn him to death, and deliver him to the Gentiles; and they will mock him, and spit upon him, and scourge him, and kill him; and after three days he will rise." In these words the course of the passion is summarily depicted in terms of a succession of events. If these statements had not been ascribed directly to Jesus but phrased in the past tense, we would recognize them at once as a report given by the Christian church after the events of Good Friday and Easter: (Jesus and his disciples) went up to Jerusalem; and the Son of man was delivered to the chief priests and the scribes, and they condemned him to death, and delivered him to the Gentiles; and they mocked him, and spat upon him, and scourged him, and killed him; and after three days he rose (from the dead). In formulating these statement as words spoken by

Jesus, however, rather than as an after-the-fact report, the intention was to stress that everything said and done by Jesus prior to Good Friday is so closely linked to the fact of his death and resurrection that it is impossible to recount his public ministry and his teaching of the disciples without constantly making explicit reference to the kerygma of Good Friday and Easter and to its intimate oneness with the whole of his life and ministry.

A further observation lends additional support to the view that in these statements we have to do not with authentic words of Jesus but with preaching and teaching in the early church. At the beginning of the passage stands the expression "Son of man." This was a Jewish title denoting sovereignty. It was employed in Jewish apocalyptic to refer to the savior who would come down from heaven in the last days to execute judgment and to liberate the righteous.[5] There is no evidence, however, that Judaism ever connected this title with suffering and death. Now it would be quite natural for us to assume that it was Jesus himself who took over this Jewish concept and gave it a wholly new meaning by establishing such a connection. But such an assumption would not be in accord with the facts, as we see them in the sources at hand. For we find the title "Son of man" used elsewhere in the Gospels in exactly the sense dictated by its Jewish origin, namely, that the Son of man will come "in the glory of his Father with the holy angels" (Mark 8:38; cf. Luke 12:8), and that they will "see the Son of man coming in clouds with great power and glory" (Mark 13:26). There is no question but what this use of the title "Son of man" with reference to the Parousia belongs to the earliest stratum of the Synoptic tradition. The change in meaning of the Jewish title, then, derives not from the historical Jesus but from the Christian church. The church took all the titles used in Judaism for describing the Messiah and applied them to Jesus in order thereby to assert that all the various hopes of salvation had

[5] See H. E. Tödt, *The Son of Man in the Synoptic Tradition*, trans. Dorothea M. Barton (London: SCM, 1965).

been fulfilled in him. Expecting the exalted Lord to appear very shortly as judge, the church proclaimed Jesus not only as the Messiah or Christ but also as the Son of man. This is why in the early Christian proclamation the title "Son of man" was linked with the suffering, death, and resurrection of Jesus. For, after all, God's anointed One was none other than the crucified One whom God had raised from death on the third day.

We thus come to the conclusion that it was the confession of the Christian church which gave form and shape to the Gospels' predictions of the passion. To assert this, however, is by no means to deny that Jesus may well have anticipated his imminent suffering and spoken about it. Statements such as those about a prophet not perishing "away from Jerusalem" (Luke 13:33) or about Jerusalem stoning "those who are sent to you" (Matt. 23:37; Luke 13:34) use phrases that do not seem to be determined by the Christian proclamation. They strongly support the assumption that Jesus did not enter upon his suffering unaware or unprepared. However, the announcement by the evangelists, solemnly repeated three times, that the Son of man would have to suffer, die, and rise is certainly not attributable in this form to Jesus himself. It was determined by the Christian interpretation of the title "Son of man" and by the manner in which Christians customarily recounted the story of the passion. For this reason these predictions of the passion can be regarded as documentary evidence concerning the earliest Christian account of the passion.

Whereas in Mark 10:33-34 the evangelist enumerates the various episodes of the passion journey sequentially, in the two preceding passion predictions he states the matter more succinctly. In Mark 9:31 we read merely that the Son of man will be delivered into the hands of men—there is a play on words involved in the coupling of the title "Son of man" with the word "men"—and the men will kill him, and then after three days he will rise. The passage in Mark 8:31 is somewhat more detailed: the Son of man must suffer many things, and be rejected by the elders and the chief priests and scribes—the reference is to the trial and condemnation by the Jewish authorities—and be killed, and after three days rise again.

In contrast to these two shorter passages, Mark 10:33-34 is particularly enlightening for our study since here the events are related in sequential fashion and an account is offered which enumerates the most important episodes in the passion story: the Son of man will be delivered—a reference to his arrest and transfer to the court of the Jewish rulers; further, they will condemn him to death—the Sanhedrin adjudged him guilty the very same night; then, they will deliver him to the Gentiles—the Jews turned Jesus over to the Roman governor Pontius Pilate to be sentenced and executed; and they will mock him, and spit upon him, and scourge him, and kill him—before the death sentence was carried out Jesus was mocked in the way Roman soldiers were accustomed to mock and maliciously abuse a condemned man before they executed him. This earliest account thus begins with the arrest of Jesus, continues with the proceeding before the Sanhedrin and the sentencing by Pontius Pilate, and concludes with the crucifixion.

What we have found out to this point about the passion of Jesus in the earliest Christian tradition can be supplemented to some extent by several passages from the Acts of the Apostles. It is a known fact that the Book of Acts includes several examples of early Christian sermons delivered on various occasions. Although these addresses were certainly not delivered in the form cited here, by Peter or any of the other apostles, there is no question but what use has been made in them of traditional materials which the author of the book has adopted and personally shaped.

It was Martin Dibelius who called attention to the fact that in these passages there is repeated reference to the death and resurrection of Christ, and that connected with this there is also repeated reference to the Old Testament ("in accordance with the scriptures" [I Cor. 15:3-5]) , and, furthermore, that the testimony adduced is always that of those who had walked with Jesus and to whom the risen One had appeared, and that at the conclusion there is always addressed to the hearers of the sermon a call to repentance and faith.[6] C. H. Dodd has confirmed these observations and proposed the thesis that from these addresses in the Book of Acts we can discover the kerygma of the early church; after all, the various sermons recorded in the first part of the book are structured almost entirely on the same pattern.[7] Several convincing observations, however, have led in more recent research to a critical view of this thesis.[8] The Old Testament quotations are never taken from the original Hebrew text, but always from the Greek translation found in the Septuagint. Furthermore, it is never stated that Christ died for our sins, something which had been so plainly stated in the early Christian confession in I Corinthians 15. Instead, we come across a number of expressions and phrases that are distinctly Lucan in style. Today therefore scholars are more strongly inclined to attribute to the author of the Book of Acts a greater share in the formulation of the substantive content of these sermons. This, of course, does not exclude the likelihood that in some passages he did make use of early tradition.

These, in brief, are the reasons why the statements in Acts must constantly be examined with a view to whether the author of Luke-Acts may have omitted something—for example, mention of the atoning death, a concept which in the case of Luke remains completely in the background— or whether here or there he may possibly have added something. It is certainly consistent with the earliest Christian proclamation that every sermon recorded in the first half of the Book of Acts mentions Jesus' cross and resurrection. This is true of Peter's sermon on the day of Pentecost (Acts 2:22

---

[6] See Dibelius, *From Tradition to Gospel, op. cit.*, pp. 9 ff.

[7] C. H. Dodd, *The Apostolic Preaching and Its Developments* (New York: Harper, 1936).

[8] See Ernst Haenchen, *Die Apostelgeschichte* (Göttingen, 1962); and Ulrich Wilckens, *Die Missionsreden der Apostelgeschichte* (2d ed.; Neukirchen, 1962).

ff.) as well as of Paul's sermon at Antioch in Pisidia (Acts 13:26 ff.). In several instances it is expressly mentioned that it was the Jews who were responsible for delivering Jesus to the Romans and that therefore they bear the greater blame for his death (Acts 2:23; 3:13-14; 5:30; 10:39; 13:27-28) ; that Pilate had wanted to set Jesus free and had freed Barabbas from prison and condemned Jesus only in response to the pleas of the Jews (Acts 3:13-14) ; and that, even though they could charge him with nothing deserving death, they had nevertheless pressured the governor to have Jesus executed (Acts 13:28). In these passages we can observe clearly that the early Christian proclamation is spurred by a desire to express loyalty toward the Roman state and as far as possible to permit no derogatory implications to be made concerning the Roman official, while at the same time assuming a polemical attitude toward the Jews who had rejected the Messiah.

Thus the relatively few statements made in Acts concerning the passion of Jesus will not serve to enrich substantially our knowledege about the earliest form of the passion story. It is essential that we hold fast instead to what we gleaned from Mark 10:33-34, which presupposes a brief account of the passion dealing with the arrest, the proceeding before the Sanhedrin, the sentencing by the Roman governor, and the crucifixion of Jesus.

That these were in fact the constituent elements in the early Christian account of Jesus' suffering can also be demonstrated by one further consideration. It is a known fact that in their portrayal of the public ministry of Jesus the Synoptics and the Gospel of John often vary greatly. While the Synoptists tell us that Jesus labored in Galilee and did not journey to Jerusalem until the very end, John informs us that the scene of his activity alternated between Galilee and Jerusalem, and that several times on the occasion of the high holy days of his people Jesus traveled up to the holy city. For all the divergence between the Synoptics and the Fourth Gospel, however, all four evangelists are in striking agreement at many points once they come to the passion story.[9] This close consensus, which commences at the start of the narrative of Jesus' suffering, can only be explained by the fact that all four evangelists base their story on an older and fixed tradition concerning the passion. John begins his account of Jesus' passion journey by reporting at once the capture of Jesus (John 18:1 ff.). Jesus has gone forth with his disciples out of Jerusalem; they have crossed the Kidron Valley and have stopped in the garden on the slope of the Mount of Olives. Then comes Judas the betrayer with the soldiers; he directs them to Jesus' nocturnal retreat that they might arrest him and lead him away. John thus presupposes an account of the passion which began with the arrest of Jesus, then told of the proceeding before the Jewish authorities and the sentencing by the governor, and dealt finally with the execution on the cross. While it is true that the fourth evangelist has for his part expanded upon this sequence of events at several points and here and there described Jesus' passion journey differently from the Synoptic writers—particularly in the impressive dialogue between Jesus and Pilate that ends with the skeptical question "What is truth?"—he nevertheless adheres to the basic framework prescribed for him by the earliest account of the passion.

Thus the comparison between John and the Synoptists confirms the analysis of Mark 10:33-34 and permits us to state the outcome of our deliberations as follows. The passion account in which the early Christian churches spoke of the suffering of their Lord began with the arrest of Jesus, continued with the proceeding before the Sanhedrin, followed with the sentencing by Pontius Pilate, and concluded with the episode of the crucifixion and death of Jesus.

But we hasten to add that the first Christians were able to relate not only this brief account but also a number of other facts relating to the passion of Jesus. Thus, for example, Paul writes in I Corinthians 11 of the instituting of the Lord's Supper, which Jesus is said to have done "on the night when he was betrayed" (I Cor. 11:23). The story of

9 See Jeremias, *The Eucharistic Words of Jesus, op. cit.,* pp. 89 ff.

the Last Supper which Jesus observed with his disciples was thus transmitted initially by word of mouth in order that the worship of the church might be ordered and conducted in accordance with the eucharistic words of Jesus. The reference to "the night" in which Jesus "was betrayed" sufficed to indicate the context in which this tradition actually belonged. The earliest account of the passion, however, as we have been trying to reconstruct it, obviously did not include the story of the Lord's last meal. Instead, the words of Jesus were repeated during the celebration of the Lord's Supper in order to perpetuate the table fellowship with Jesus through the remembrance of Christ's atoning death and through confession of the risen and exalted Lord. If in the case of Mark—and correspondingly in the case of the two other Synoptists—the pericope of the institution of the Lord's Supper has found its place within the narrative of the passion story, this is because the evangelist himself has simply taken this particular tradition, which at first circulated independently, and has incorporated it into the account of the passion, thereby assuring it a firm place within the gospel.

To cite a second example, the same is true of the story of the anointing of Jesus at Bethany, which is reported not only by the Synoptists but also by John, in every case with the interpretation that the homage paid by the woman is an anticipation of the anointing of Jesus for burial. In this connection Luke represents an exception. He does not speak of an anointing in connection with the passion but presents a similar story in a much earlier context. Jesus is a guest in the home of a Pharisee when a woman enters, stands before him, wets his feet with her tears and wipes them with the hair of her head, kisses his feet and anoints them with precious ointment (Luke 7:36-50). Originally this too was an independent piece of tradition, which need not have been connected with Jesus' passion journey. It is only by way of the last two verses appended by Mark (14:8-9) and Matthew (26:12-13)—as well as by John (12:7-8)—in which reference is made to Jesus' death and burial that this story has been incorporated into the passion narrative.

The original brief version of the oldest passion tradition was thus enlarged by taking up individual stories then in circulation and incorporating them into the broader framework. What this means is that the passion story has been expanded beyond where it originally began, so that in our Gospels the account of Jesus' passion journey begins not with his arrest but as far back as Mark 14:1, with the decision of the Jewish authorities to do away with him as soon as possible. In fact, the evangelist has pushed the framework of the passion story back even beyond that by beginning his eleventh chapter with the entry of Jesus into Jerusalem and using that to inaugurate the sequence of events covering the last days Jesus spent in the holy city.

At the conclusion of his account of Jesus' activity in Galilee, however, the evangelist Mark has placed a single sentence which is intended to give to all readers of his book a clue as to the vantage point from which the subsequent narrative is to be read and understood: "For the Son of man also came not to be served but to serve, and to give his life as a ransom for many" (Mark 10:45). This, then, is the service which Jesus has performed for all. He has paid the ransom for our redemption. To put it once again in the terminology of the earliest Christian confession, he has died for our sins.

2.

Jesus' Entry into Jerusalem and the Cleansing of the Temple

Coming from Jericho, Jesus journeys with his disciples up to Jerusalem. The road begins in the depths of the Jordan Valley and runs through desolate country up to the heights of the Judean hills—along the route which was the locale of the action described in the Parable of the Good Samaritan. The evangelist Mark gives no reason for this trip to the holy city. He merely states that the Son of man must suffer and die in Jerusalem. This "must," repeated in the three predictions of Christ's passion (Mark 8:31; 9:31; 10:33 -34), is not an expression of the inexorability of fate but points rather to the fact that in the passion of Christ it is the will of God that is to be fulfilled. The Christian church could understand the suffering of Christ in no other way: that the Messiah should be given over unto death had been ordained by the hidden plan and decree of God. The evangelists offer no other explanation; and if we were to try to suggest reasons for Jesus' going from Galilee to Judea and travelling to Jerusalem for the Passover, they would all be a matter of pure conjecture. In Luke 13:33 we are told that Jesus said a prophet must die in Jerusalem. This saying suggests that Jesus may have seen his own course prefigured in the fate suffered by the prophets before him. As they had been persecuted and rejected in Jerusalem, so in his case must the issue be decided in Jerusalem.

The larger narrative dealing with the last days of Jesus begins with the story of his entry into Jerusalem with his disciples. Included in this section are a number of quite diverse items which are only loosely connected. But the more nearly the account approaches the end, the more precise becomes the sequence of events described by the evangelists. Most exact of all is the information concerning the day of execution. Mark mentions first the morning (15:1), then the third hour (15:25), and then the sixth hour (15:33); Mark 15:34 specifies the ninth hour as the time of Jesus' death, and according to Mark 15:42 it was late in the day when he was laid in the grave.

Using these stipulations as a starting point and keeping in mind the time references made previously, we get a clear picture of the chronological framework within which Mark has set his description of the many happenings there in Jerusalem. The evening before the day of execution, that is, during the night from Thursday to Friday—for the day following the crucifixion was a sabbath (Mark 15:42; Luke 23:54; John 19:31)—Jesus partook of his last meal with his disciples. That same night he stopped in Gethsemane, was arrested, and brought before the Sanhedrin which turned him over to the Roman governor early the next morning. Mark 14:1 says that the Passover and the Feast of Unleavened Bread was to be observed two days hence. This means that the decision of the Jewish authorities to do away with Jesus must have been made on Wednesday; the story of the anointing is also set on the same day. At the point where he begins the narrative about the controversial discourses of Jesus and his apocalyptic sayings, Mark mentions that it was early in the day (11:20), that is, early on Tuesday. According to Mark 11:12, the cursing of the fig tree took place on the preceding day, that is, on Monday. Since this episode followed by one day Christ's entry into Jerusalem, the entry must have taken place on the first day of the week. Thus the chronological framework spans the time from Palm Sunday through Good Friday to Easter morning. The evangelist

Mark has thus encompassed all the events of Jesus' passion within the days of this one week. This chronological sequence of events is accordingly to be attributed to the editorial hand of the evangelist, who took the various traditions available to him and combined them with the brief passion account to form one large connected narrative.

The story of the passion begins with a geographical reference which itself is not clear: "When they drew near to Jerusalem, to Bethphage and Bethany, at the Mount of Olives. . . . " (Mark 11:1). Bethphage is located just east of Jerusalem, right on the city limits, while Bethany is a short distance away from Jerusalem on the southeastern slope of the Mount of Olives. In Jesus' day the road, built by the Romans, took a somewhat different route from that whereby one reaches Jerusalem today. In those days the route did not run through Bethany but bypassed it on the right, heading straight toward Bethphage and then on to Jerusalem. The geographical designation in Mark's Gospel, therefore, cannot possibly be correct. It must have been recorded by someone who was not completely familiar with the geography in and around Jerusalem. We might surmise that the oral tradition had spoken at first only about Bethphage, but that the name of Bethany was soon added because of the greater importance this town had for the first Christians. Bethany is where Mary and Martha lived. It was also the site of the raising of Lazarus. And it was here that Jesus had lodged during those last nights when he sought seclusion from the city so overcrowded with Passover pilgrims. The evangelist correctly locates Bethany at the foot of the Mount of Olives. The location is expressly stipulated, possibly because according to Jewish expectation the Mount of Olives was to be the site where the God of Israel would appear in order to deliver Jerusalem and execute judgment upon his enemies (Zech. 14:4-5). It was also on the Mount of Olives that the Messiah was to come forth to effect the liberation of Israel. The Messiah whose entry the evangelist Mark is now about to describe, however, comes not as a victorious ruler hurling his enemies to the ground but as the Servant of God entering upon his suffering.

Arriving at the outskirts of Jerusalem, Jesus sends two of his disciples on ahead charged with a specific commission. They are to enter the village before them, and every detail of what will transpire there is told them in advance. They will find a colt tied, on which no one has ever sat. They are to untie it and bring it. And if anyone should object, they are to answer, "The Lord has need of it " (Mark 11:3). He will then have no more misgivings, but will surrender the animal to them. Everything happens as Jesus foretold it. The disciples go on ahead and carry out Jesus' instructions. The mention of the tethered colt is presumably an allusion to Genesis 49:11. In this verse, which Judaism interpreted messianically, we read that Judah would bind "his foal to the vine and his ass's colt to the choice vine." The tethered colt on which no one has ever sat is taken to be a mount for the Messiah. Since it is unblemished it fills the requirements for being a sacred animal.

The evangelist Matthew (21:3-7) specifically calls attention to a passage from Zechariah 9:9, according to which the messianic king will ride on an ass and on a colt, the foal of an ass. The twin expression in this Old Testament passage, which is simply a matter of poetic parallelism, obviously has reference only to a single animal, here designated by two words. The rabbinically trained evangelist, however, attaches great importance to the fact that the words of prophecy have been fulfilled to the letter. As a result, without pausing to consider how uncomfortable such a ride could be, he simply remarks that Jesus actually sat on two animals.

Jesus rides into the city on this animal which the disciples had brought him, which they had covered with their garments. Many of the people lining the path spread their garments on the road, others bring leafy branches which they had cut from the fields, and together they pay homage to Jesus. The crowds that precede and that follow break out in the cry of jubilation: "Hosanna! Blessed is he who comes

in the name of the Lord! Blessed is the kingdom of our
father David that is coming! Hosanna in the highest!" (Mark
11:9-10).[1]

These words have reference to Psalm 118:25-26, though
the entering one is here understood to be the messianic king
to whom homage is paid rather than, as in the Old Testament, the group of pilgrims coming into the temple. The
verses from Psalm 118 are not quoted verbatim but are altered in characteristic fashion, not only by the strange mention of "the kingdom of our father David that is coming" but
also by the repetition of the hosanna cry—it is repeated
as a summons to praise in the heavenly heights. In Matthew
too we find not a literal quotation but a free adaptation of
the Psalm words. "The kingdom of our father David that is
coming"—which was not a common expression in Judaism
—is omitted and the cry of hosanna is directed to the Son
of David (Matt 21:9). As in Mark, there is a concluding
appeal for jubilation in the heights of heaven. While Luke
19:38 skips the cry of hosanna—which would hardly be
meaningful to Hellenistic readers—and echoes Psalm 118:26
only very faintly, the Fourth Gospel in its brief description of
the entry of Jesus into Jerusalem employs at the beginning
the same words used in Mark 11:9: "Hosanna! Blessed is he
who comes in the name of the Lord" (John 12:13). The
messianic significance of the Old Testament phrase is then
unequivocally asserted in the words that follow: " . . . even
the King of Israel!"

The cry of hosanna, found in all Four Gospels at this
same point, yet nowhere else in the New Testament, must
have been firmly imbedded in the earliest Christian tradition. It was intimately connected with the liturgical tradition
of Judaism. During the Jewish high holy days of Passover
and Tabernacles it was sung by the festive throngs as a part
of the Hallel Psalms (Psalms 113-118). In this connection,
pre-Christian Judaism had already ceased to interpret the

---

[1] On this passage and the discussion here following, see Eduard Lohse,
"Hosianna," *Novum Testament*, VI (1963), 113-119.

hosanna as a plea for help—Save, O Lord—and had understood it rather as an exultant homage intended to point
to the one who should and would come in the name of the
Lord. Christians simply took up the expression and used it
to confess their faith in Jesus as the Messiah.

By concluding the story of Jesus' entry into Jerusalem
with the exclamatory hosanna in which the great multitude
joins, the evangelist Mark is obviously placing special stress
on this word. This emphasis, however, must not be understood in terms of what the Jewish festival pilgrims were
thinking about as they journeyed with Jesus to Jerusalem.
For it is not Mark's intention at all to present here merely
a historical report. His purpose is rather, even at the very
beginning of his larger narrative of Jesus' last days and journey to the cross, to emphasize just who this Christ is who
thus enters into suffering. The evangelist mentions "the
kingdom of our father David that is coming" in order thereby to declare that in this Lord now walking toward the cross
the whole of God's history with Israel finds its fulfillment
and culmination.

The same thing may be seen even more clearly in the
Gospel of Matthew. Here the cry of jubilation is addressed
to the Son of David (Matt. 21:9-15). Jesus is thereby designated as the Messiah promised to Israel, who comes in the
name of the Lord. With this word from Psalm 118:25-26
the evangelist points beyond the passion of Christ to his return in glory—to the Parousia. For in Matthew 23:39 (cf.
Luke 13:35) the same Psalm verse recurs, though this time
in connection with the word of judgment spoken against a
Jerusalem hardened in unbelief. Jesus shall return for judgment, and then everyone will have to understand and say,
"Blessed is he who comes in the name of the Lord." When
that time comes no one will be able any longer to deny to
the Lord that honor which was withheld from the humiliated Servant of God.

That the hosanna cry must be understood in terms of
the eschatological expectation of the early Christians is con-

firmed by its use in the worship life of the early church. In *The Teaching of the Twelve Apostles* we read the words spoken at the beginning of the celebration of the Lord's Supper: "Let Grace come and let this world pass away. Hosanna to the God of David! If anyone is holy, let him come. If not, let him repent. Our Lord, come! Amen."[2] The eschatological thrust of these phrases is evident. What is prayed for is the passing away of this world and the coming of the Lord. With its hosanna, the confessing church reaches out toward the Lord. It is confident of his coming for it knows him as the One who has come. The words which Hegesippus cites in the legendary account of the martyrdom of James, the brother of the Lord, are full of this same hope for the Parousia. Hegesippus writes that James referred to Jesus as the One who is seated in heaven at the right hand of Power and who will come on the clouds of heaven. In response to this testimony many who heard his words burst forth with the jubilant words of praise: "Hosanna to the Son of David."[3]

From the very beginnings of the Christian church the hosanna has always had its place in the liturgy of the Lord's Supper. It is sung as a joyful confession brought to the coming Lord. In adopting this liturgically oriented cry of Judaism and using it to confess their faith in the Messiah, the earliest Christians intended to point out that the Son of David is not a sovereign who will rule in Jerusalem and restore the glory of the Davidic kingdom; he is the crucified Servant of God who has come in the name of the Lord, and in the name of the Lord will come to make his triumphal entry as the anointed One of God.

Inasmuch as the story of Jesus' entry into Jerusalem is also found in John (12:12-15), in a brief form that is independent of the Synoptics and in which both Psalm 118:25-26 and Zechariah 9:9 are specifically quoted, it can be stated with assurance that this particular tradition must have been

---

2 Didache 10:6; trans. Cyril C. Richardson (Library of Christian Classics, Vol. I [Philadelphia: Westminster, 1953]), p. 176.

3 Eusebius *Ecclesiastical History* ii. 23, 13-14.

known already to Mark as a tradition of earlier origin. The fact that Mark has placed the event at the very beginning of his entire passion narrative indicates that this arrangement is the result of a conscious decision on his part. For in John we come across a different sequence of events. First, there is the anointing of Jesus, and only after that do we hear of the entry of Jesus on the following day as he journeys from Bethany to Jerusalem (John 12:1-9). By starting out with the story of the entry and placing impressively at its conclusion the cry of hosanna, Mark for his part is indicating that the characteristic features of the coming Lord are already portrayed in the figure of this Jesus now entering Jerusalem. The person who reads subsequently about the suffering and humiliation of Jesus must never forget that the crucified One is none other than the risen and exalted One who shall come to judge the living and the dead.

The fact that Jesus' journey ends at the temple suggests that as he comes up from the Kidron Valley he enters the holy area through one of the temple gates. However, after a brief look around he again leaves the temple area and returns with the twelve to Bethany in order to spend the night there (Mark 11:11). This represents a strange break in the continuity of the Marcan account, for one would have expected Jesus to go into action at once, as in fact he is reported to have done by both Matthew (21:12) and Luke (19:45). Presumably Mark introduced the caesura at this point so as to be able to distribute the various events over all the days of the holy week and thus preserve his chronological framework.

Matthew and Luke both depart from this apparently artificial arrangement. In their accounts the entry into Jerusalem is followed immediately by the story of Jesus' appearance in the temple. Each one, however, interposes a brief passage derived from his own independent source.

According to Matthew (21:10-11), upon his arrival in Jerusalem Jesus causes a great stir among all the people who greet him as the prophet from Nazareth. He then goes at once to the temple, where he not only effects its cleansing but also heals the lame and the blind who crowd about him, and receives homage and praise out of the mouths of children (Matt. 21:14-17). The Servant of God bears the sickness and suffering of many, and is surrounded by the poor and humble people who constitute his true church.

Luke, on the other hand, has Jesus the moment he enters immediately warn of impending judgment because Jerusalem has refused to recognize the appointed time of its visitation (Luke 19:39-44). According to Luke, Jesus does not actually enter the city, but goes directly to the temple.[4] He remains at a certain distance from the city proper, and does not actually enter Jerusalem until he is about to partake of the last meal with his disciples (Luke 22:7-10). He takes possession of the temple because this is the place where from of old God has been worshiped and sought in prayer. At the beginning of the Gospel there was talk about the temple, where Zechariah served at the altar (Luke 1:5-23). And at the close Luke has another reference to the temple: the disciples to whom the risen One has appeared "were continually in the temple blessing God" (Luke 24:53). Thus it is the temple, the holy place of Israel, that serves as a link between the band of the disciples and God's people of the old covenant. The temple is no longer the place that rightfully belongs to the Jews, however; it is now the site where the disciples of Jesus, who have experienced the fulfillment of the Old Testament prophecies, raise their voices in praise of God. It is in Jesus that the shift from the old to the new takes place. It is he, together with his disciples, who makes the temple once again a place for the true worship of God.

With reference to the Psalm 118 and Zechariah 9 passages we have been discussing, the fourth evangelist remarks in his version of the entry that it was not until Jesus was glorified that these words were understood by his disciples: "Then

---

[4] See Hans Conzelmann, *The Theology of St. Luke*, trans. Geoffrey Buswell (New York: Harper, 1960), esp. pp. 73-80, 132-139; and Eduard Lohse, "Zion-Jerusalem im Neuen Testament," in *Theologisches Wörterbuch zum Neuen Testament, op. cit.*, VII, 330 ff.

they remembered that this had been written of him and had been done to him" (John 12:16). Not until after Easter could the disciples really assess what had happened at the time. Only then do they see in the humiliated One the glorified One, who is the Lord of his people. By this comment the evangelist shows that all the reports subsequently given by the church concerning the deeds of Jesus and his journey to the cross must necessarily have been shaped from the perspective of the post-Easter church. For without belief in and confession of the exalted Christ it is quite impossible to understand what once transpired.

Basic to the account of Jesus' entry into Jerusalem, which each evangelist has given in his own way in order to emphasize what to him seemed most important, is the undoubtedly historical fact that Jesus went with his disciples to Jerusalem and there met his death. But it is hardly conceivable that a triumphal entry into the holy city of the Jews could have occurred without immediately arousing the suspicion of the Roman occupying powers and provoking them to some kind of action. We might therefore picture the historical event in terms of a teacher riding on a donkey while his pupils walked along beside him on foot—a sight that was not at all uncommon in Palestine. It is possible that the arrival of a teacher as famous as the prophet from Nazareth did create a bit of a stir. But merely to set forth such facts would have been of no interest whatever to the Christian church. The church instead formulated the account of Jesus' entry in such a way as to make it a scene of triumph. The Lord commands and all do his bidding. He is the one whom the people honor with their joyous greetings and cries of hosanna. As then he came in the name of the Lord, so will he in the same name also return at the Parousia.

The Synoptic Gospels combine the entry of Jesus with the cleansing of the temple. The two pericopes belong closely together. In the case of Mark (11:12-21) the passage dealing with the cleansing of the temple is framed by the story of the cursing of the fig tree and the discourse of the following

day concerning that same fig tree now withered away to its
roots. This story, which probably represents an elaboration
of the parable of the barren fig tree (Luke 13:6-9), is intended to underscore the seriousness of the judgment that
awaits Jerusalem. It does interrupt, however, the original
sequence of the two closely related passages of Jesus' entry
and his subsequent cleansing of the temple.

With his disciples Jesus proceeds to the temple area. Without a single word of preliminary description or preparation,
it is suddenly stated that Jesus casts out all within the temple
area who buy or sell and that he overturns the tables of the
money changers and the seats of those who sell pigeons. The
confusion and bustle there in the forecourt of the temple
was part and parcel of the ordinary routine connected with
the temple cult of sacrifice and with the presence of so many
festival pilgrims. Since the Jews who had come long distances
to the temple were not able to bring a sacrificial animal
along on their journey, it was necessary for them to be able
to purchase at the holy place itself an umblemished animal
which they could then offer as a sacrifice. From time im-
memorial only Tyrian currency was acceptable in the temple
area. Since the pilgrims did not possess such currency they
were obliged to exchange the coins they had with them for
money that would be valid in the temple. This is why the
money changers had been given permission by the priesthood
to take up their places in the forecourt of the temple. The
vendors offered doves at a cheap price so that even poor
people could bring at least some small offering to the altar.
Apparently no one took offence at these dealings that transpired daily in the temple area.

The severity of Jesus' attack is reminiscent of the sharp
criticism once leveled by the Old Testament prophets against
the practices of the temple cult. Thus Jeremiah reproached
his generation with the word of the Lord: "Has this house,
which is called by my name, become a den of robbers in your
eyes?" (Jer. 7:11). The prophet is objecting to the abuses
practiced by men who want merely to use the cult for their

own selfish ends.   Jesus' cleansing of the temple is also to be interpreted as a prophetic and symbolic action; this is expressly stated in the words: "Is it not written, 'My house shall be called a house of prayer for all the nations'? But you have made it a den of robbers" (Mark 11:17). Both Isaiah 56:7 and Jeremiah 7:11 are incorporated in this passage, and the emphasis is on the fact that the temple, intended to be a place of prayer, has been desecrated by the now customary hubbub and bustle. This word represents an attack not only on the vendors and money changers who get thrown out, but primarily on the people actually responsible for these daily practices in the temple area. The chief priests, evidently realizing that they are the real object of the attack, decide to do away with Jesus; only their fear of the crowds that cling to him restrains them for the moment from implementing the decision (Mark 11:18).

The fourth evangelist too reports that Jesus cleansed the temple. He does not link the incident to Jesus' last days in Jerusalem, however, but places it at the very beginning of Jesus' public ministry. This shift is obviously at variance with the historical background of the story. Its purpose is simply to indicate in an almost programmatic way that in his public ministry Jesus becomes involved in a life and death struggle with the Jews, who are here actually portrayed as types or representatives of the unbelieving cosmos. The fourth evangelist does not speak only of the cleansing of the holy place by the expulsion of the money changers and those who sold sacrificial animals. He goes beyond the Synoptists to add that Jesus also cast out the sheep and the oxen (John 2:15). To drive out the sacrificial animals as well was surely tantamount to an attack on the sacificial cult itself. Undoubtedly John wanted to stress that true worship was to be found no longer in connection with the temple cult, but only where the Father is worshiped in spirit and in truth (cf. John 4:24). This criticism, however, which calls in question the validity and worth of the whole temple apparatus, takes John beyond the position of the other evangelists—and certainly also beyond the realm of historical fact.

The Johannine pericope of the cleansing of the temple is followed by a brief dispute between Jesus and the Jewish authorities in which they ask him what sign he can show them to indicate his authority for doing this (John 2:18). According to the Synoptists too, the question is put to Jesus as to the authority by which he does this, which in effect is a demand that he justify his conduct (Matt. 21:23; Mark 11:28; Luke 20:2). The answer given to this challenging question by the Synoptists is different from that of John. In both instances, however, Jesus' answer consists not in a direct response to their challenge, but in a statement which, while seeming formally to be a direct answer, is actually a rejection of the question. In the tradition available to the evangelists, therefore, a firm connection must have existed between the cleansing of the temple and the question concerning Jesus' authority, a connection which presumably had its origin in the historical event of the cleansing of the temple. The answer Jesus gives to the Jews in John 2:19 also fits into this same context: "Destroy this temple, and in three days I will raise it up (again)."[5] Just as the Jews anticipated that when the Messiah came the temple would be restored in new splendor and glory, so also does this Jesus logion point to the imminent dawning of the age of salvation. The fourth evangelist, to be sure, has already reformulated the terminology about destroying and raising up, or resurrecting, with a view to the subsequent interpretation. For he relates the destruction and raising of the temple to the temple of Jesus' body, to his death and his resurrection after three days (John 2:21). That what is involved here is a secondary meaning added to the original word of Jesus is quite apparent. The ironic challenge to the Jews that they should themselves lay hands on the holy place is meant to suggest that because of their rejection of Jesus they themselves are

[5] On Mark 14:58 and parallel passages see pages 83-84 below.

responsible for the temple's being reduced to dust and ashes forty years after the death of Jesus.

A comparison of the Synoptic and Johannine versions of the cleansing of the temple shows that the discussion concerning Jesus' authority was closely connected with the event that preceded it. The story makes clear that the altercation between Jesus and the Jewish authorities is now culminating in a conflict of deadly seriousness. The decision which they have taken against Jesus stands firm; now they must find a favorable opportunity to implement it. The action moves quickly toward its climax. But before the *via dolorosa* of Jesus is described in detail, the evangelist Mark —Matthew and Luke follow his lead in this—interjects a sizable section dealing with the controversies between Jesus and the chief priests, scribes, and elders, the Pharisees and Sadducees (Mark 11:27—12:40). In chapter 13 there follows Jesus' address to his disciples concerning the events that are to transpire at the end of time. The coming of the Son of man will be preceded by frightful terrors and by grave perils for the church. His coming, however, is certain. The apocalyptic discourse which has been moved to this position is intended to remind the reader once more that the suffering Servant of God will appear as the Son of man to judge the unbelievers and to set free his people.[6] The course he follows is according to the plan and decree of God. The cross, however, is followed by Easter. The expectation of the Son of man points beyond his suffering to the sovereign rule which the exalted One will exercise at the right hand of God, and which he will make manifest at the end of days. Whatever may happen, there can be no doubt of the victory of Jesus Christ.

Having prepared his readers in this manner for a proper understanding of the passion story, Mark returns again in 14:11ff. to the decision—already mentioned in 11:18— which the Jewish authorities had taken against Jesus. They

[6] See R. H. Lightfoot, *The Gospel Message of St. Mark* (2d ed., Oxford: Clarendon, 1952), pp. 39-40, 48.

want to kill him, but without the attendant publicity which would certainly occur if they were to lay hands on him publicly. This is why they say, "Not during the feast" (Mark 14:2). Instead Jesus is to be seized secretly and then quickly dispatched. This plan is facilitated by Judas' willing offer to help them apprehend Jesus at night outside the city (Mark 14:10-11). Mark declines to suggest any motive for Judas' betrayal. He says nothing about a disillusioned messianic expectation, nor about the greed which for a miserable reward led Judas to commit this shameful act. Although it was not long before such explanations were given, the evangelist himself does not try to illumine the agonizing darkness which envelops the enigmatic behavior of one of the twelve. It is by virtue of God's own plan and wisdom, so very hidden to human eyes, that the Son of man is to be abandoned to utter desolation, betrayed by one of his own trusted ones—in order that he might drain to the very dregs the cup of suffering.

3.

The Institution of the
Lord's Supper

The tradition about the Last Supper which Jesus shared with his desciples was preserved and passed down by the early Christians in connection with the celebration of the Lord's Supper in the worship services of the church. Paul is the first to record this tradition, which consists of but a few sentences. In the eleventh chapter of his First Letter to the Corinthians he quotes the words of institution in order to correct the from of the celebration which had fallen into disorder at Corinth. The apostle introduces this quotation with words similar to those used to introduce the kerygma concerning the death and resurrection of Christ: "he received from the Lord" what he "also delivered" to the Corinthians, namely, "that the Lord Jesus on the night when he was betrayed took bread," etc.

When Paul states here that he received it "from the Lord" this can hardly mean that he heard these sentences spoken directly by the exalted Lord. Although some exegetes have tried to interpret the passage in this sense,[1] such an interpretation can hardly be taken seriously, especially since Paul here employs the same terms that he used in I Corinthians 15:3 (received—delivered) . These were the same words Jewish scribes used to designate the reception and transmission of a tradition which was passed on from one generation to an-

[1] See, e.g., Hans Lietzmann, *An die Korinther* I/II (3d ed.; Tübingen, 1931), p. 57; and *idem, Mass and Lord's Supper*, trans. Dorothea H. G. Reeve (Leiden: Brill, 1953—   ), p. 208.

other: "Moses received the torah from Sinai and delivered it to Joshua, and Joshua to the elders, and the elders to the prophets, and the prophets delivered it to the men of the Great Synagogue."[2] Paul too undoubtedly has in mind here a tradition which is continually passed on by word of mouth within the Christian church. This particular tradition, however, is no longer connected with the authority attached to the names of famous scribes, and is certainly not traced back to the giving of the law at Sinai. Instead, Paul names the authority from whom every word of Christian teaching and preaching receives its validity: "from the Lord."[3] What is to be heard in the sentences transmitted is the word of the Lord himself. Thus these sentences do not merely repeat a report of events that once transpired and now belong to the past. On the contrary, they are intended to attest that it is this same Lord who in the celebration of his Supper is presently acting here and now on behalf of and in fellowship with his assembled church.

The writers of the Gospels presuppose this particular tradition about the Last Supper, but they have incorporated it firmly within the larger context of the passion story. This is why we do not find in the Gospels, as in Paul, an introductory statement referring to the reception and transmission of the tradition. The evangelists instead write everything in the form of a report, setting before the pericope about the Supper's institution a lengthy introduction which is intended to afford the pericope its proper locus and to establish the context within which it is to be interpreted. Of course, we can still see very easily that the verses which speak of the institution of the Supper originally formed a single, independent, and self-contained unit unrelated to anything that preceded or followed. In Mark 14:22 we read: "And as they were eating, he took bread." The little phrase "And as they were eating" establishes a loose connection within the larger con-

[2] Mishna Aboth 1:1.

[3] K. Wegenast, *Das Verständnis der Tradition bei Paulus und den Deuteropaulinen* (Neukirchen, 1962).

text. Yet in the light of what precedes, such an introduction would hardly have been necessary. For, in 14:18, Mark had already written: "And as they were at table eating, Jesus said." We thus see that in referring to the setting for the Supper the evangelist uses almost the very same words twice and in quick succession. What this means is that in the passion story as told by Mark and the other evangelists a number of disconnected fragments have been strung together and so integrated by way of introductions as to constitute one continuous narrative.

At the beginning it is reported that Jesus sent two of his disciples on ahead to make the necessary preparations for the Passover celebration for him and his band of disciples. The evangelist introduces this account with a strange time reference: "And on the first day of Unleavened Bread, when they sacrificed the passover lamb" (Mark 14:12). On closer examination these words are seen to contain a contradiction. Within Judaism the Feast of Unleavened Bread had become closely associated with the Feast of the Passover. In remembrance of the exodus of Israel from Egypt the Jews ate no leavened bread for seven days. This was because the Old Testament related that the departure of Israel was so hurried that there was no time for leavening the bread. In commemoration of the exodus all leftovers of leavened bread in every Jewish household are removed before the Passover, and the Feast is observed with sweet breads. The additional phrase which Mark appends—"when they sacrificed the passover lamb"—is obviously intended to identify more precisely that "first day." But herein lies the contradiction. For the slaughter of the paschal lambs did not take place on the "first day" of the Feast but on the preceding day, the Day of Preparation. And this is the only day that could be meant here, for it is supposed to be a question of getting ready for the Passover. Thus the phrase that speaks of the first day of Unleavened Bread is very inaccurate to say the least, if not downright false. For no Jew versed in the law would have spoken of the first day of the festival when he really meant the Day of Preparation.[4]

It is necessary to call special attention to this contradiction in the introductory time reference because a deduction affecting our judgment of the entire pericope can be drawn from it. The author of these sentences was not a Jewish Christian from Palestine, for such a person would certainly have been able to distinguish clearly between the Feast itself and the Day of Preparation. The sentences must have been formulated rather in a Hellenistic milieu where people were not altogether familiar with Jewish festival customs. What we have here then is not a historical report, but a later composition intended as an introduction to the older tradition about the Last Supper, an introduction which could serve to establish and emphasize the connection between the Supper and the Passover.

Mark states that Jesus sent two of his disciples on ahead to make the required preparations in Jerusalem, but Mark does not give us their names (Mark 14:13). In Luke 22:8 we read that it was Peter and John who were thus commissioned. Since the evangelists frequently mention Peter and John as especially intimate disciples of Jesus, Luke—whose account is later than that of Mark—interjects their name at this point as well. But since Luke had no more direct and detailed knowledge of the course of these events than Mark, what we have here is an instance of something that happens repeatedly: a later narrator, in an effort to add greater color to the account found in his original source, will retroactively add the names of persons who had formerly gone unnamed. It can readily be seen that even the stories narrated by Mark have been augmented here and there in this manner.

The two disciples are told that a man carrying a jar of water will meet them; they are to follow him, and where he enters they are to say to the householder, "The Teacher says, Where is my guest room, where I am to eat the passover with

my disciples?" (Mark 14:13-14; Luke 22:10-11; Matt. 26:18).
Then everything immediately happens as Jesus foretold it.
As in the story of the entry into Jerusalem (Mark 11:2-7)
the evangelist here again makes use of a legendary motif
found also in the Old Testament. In I Samuel 10:2 ff., for
example, we read that Samuel anointed Saul to be king and
told him in detail whom he would meet on his way and what
would then transpire. As Saul proceeds on his way the prediction is fulfilled to the letter. In stressing these words of
Jesus and their immediate fulfillment the evangelist is en-
deavoring to say that events of a wondrous nature occurred.
The person now readying himself to sit at table with his
disciples is the Lord himself; all men must be at his service
in order that his journey may be completed.

If we take into account these motifs that shape the evangelist's narrative we shall cease trying to regard his report as
an exact historical rendition of what actually happened at
the time. We shall realize instead that what the evangelist is
here trying to do is to proclaim a message, to make certain
theologically significant statements. Jesus' Last Supper is to
be viewed in terms of the Passover meal which is now being
supplanted by the Lord's Supper. Christ's church no longer
observes the feasts of the old covenant. It confesses instead its
faith in its Lord, who for our sake was nailed to the cross.
Jesus is the Lord who commands, and whose words are un-
conditionally obeyed.

How Jesus' orders to the disciples were fulfilled is reported
with the single brief statement that "they prepared the passover" (Mark 14:16; Matt. 26:19; Luke 22:13). As part of the
preparation for the Feast it was necessary that the room in
which the Feast was to take place be thoroughly searched to
cleanse it of any traces of leavened bread, and that in the
afternoon of the Day of Preparation a Passover lamb be
slaughtered at the temple and readied for the festival meal.
The large number of pilgrims who came to Jerusalem for
the Passover often outnumbered by far the local inhabitants
of the city. Since all participants at the Feast, however, had

to eat the Passover meal within the walls of Jerusalem, all citizens of the city were required to take the pilgrims into their own homes. The account in the Synoptic Gospels accordingly presupposes that the disciples of Jesus were able to find a room in one of the houses of the city where Jesus could celebrate the Passover with them.

In Mark and Matthew the account of the meal begins with the identification of the traitor. Luke, on the other hand, observes a different sequence. In his account it is not until after the words of institution that Jesus speaks of the betrayal by Judas. Inasmuch as in this portion of the passion story Luke presents a quite different sequence of events, as well as several strongly divergent formulations, we must reckon with the possibility that in this section he is relying not on Mark but on some other source, whose precise nature and form have been the object of thorough research on the part of many scholars.[5] At this point it is of course not possible to discuss in detail the special problems related to the Lucan tradition. Suffice it to say that in the case of all the evangelists (cf. John 13:18-20) the story of the meal is connected —though in varying sequences—with the identification of the traitor.

In this episode the Passover setting is not mentioned. It is simply stated that Jesus is at table eating with his disciples. It is only the connection with what preceded that makes the reader think of the Passover meal. Jesus turns to his disciples and says that one of them will betray him. In reply to their frightened question as to who this would be, he says "It is . . . one who is dipping bread in the same dish with me" (Mark 14:20). Mark does not directly quote here from the Old Testament, though all three Synoptists would clearly

---

[5] Concerning the sources used by Luke see Burnett Hillman Streeter, *The Four Gospels: A Study of Origins* (London: Macmillan, 1924); Adolf Schlatter, *Das Evangelium des Lukas* (Stuttgart, 1931); Bultmann, *The History of the Synoptic Tradition, op. cit.,* pp. 279-280; Heinz Schürmann, *Quellenkritische Untersuchung des Lukanischen Abendmahlsberichtes* (3 vols.; Münster, 1953–1957); Friedrich Rehkopf *Die Lukanische Sonderquelle* (Tübingen; Mohr, 1959); Jeremias, *The Eucharistic Words of Jesus, op. cit.,* pp. 97 ff.

remind us of the word from the Psalms which John 13:18 specifically mentions: "who ate of my bread, has lifted his heel against me" (Ps. 41:9). How was it possible for one who belonged to the circle of Christ's most intimate friends to become a traitor? The enormity of this ignominious betrayal cannot be understood at all except in the light of Scripture. In the Psalms it was foretold that one out of the fellowship of friends would become the traitor. Since the Christian church sought to interpret the passion in terms of the Scriptures, the words of Scripture also played a role in the shaping of the tradition. Psalm 41:9 makes plain why the announcement of the betrayal would have to take place during a common meal. On these presuppositions it is clear why there should have arisen this picture of Jesus sitting with his disciples at the moment when he identifies the traitor. The anxious and worried question which the disciples put to Jesus points beyond the immediate situation. It has been so formulated by the evangelists that every Christian should hear it as an admonition to personal self-examination: "Is it I?" (Mark 14:19; Matt. 26:22).

The passage dealing with the problem of the betrayal and surrender of Jesus concludes with a saying which at first was certainly transmitted independently but then soon came to be connected with the identification of the traitor: "For the Son of man goes as it is written of him, but woe to that man by whom the Son of man is betrayed! It would have been better for that man if he had not been born" (Mark 14:21; Matt. 26:24; Luke 22:22). The Semitic character of this statement—notably the twofold use of the term "Son of man" followed by the twofold repetition of the term "man" —is clear evidence that it was originally formulated by the earliest Palestinian Christians. The same reasons given in connection with our discussion of the title "Son of man"[6] argue validly here too against the notion that this saying may have originated with the historical Jesus. The connection between the Son of man and suffering was first estab-

6 See pp. 12-13 above.

lished in later Christian teaching and preaching. The Christian church believed and confessed that it was the will of God that the anointed One should be handed over, forsaken, and betrayed. Yet this inscrutable plan and decree of God does not nullify the responsibility and guilt of him who shamefully does the betraying. Punishment and judgment will overtake him. Hence it is written, "It would have been better for that man if he had not been born."

Our deliberations to this point have shown that both the pericope of the preparation for the Feast of the Passover as well as the episode involving the identification of the traitor represent later segments that clearly reflect the influence of the church's teaching and preaching. The framework which the evangelist has constructed around the brief tradition of the words of institution must therefore be viewed as his own creation, effected in conjunction with his use of various motifs and statements from the tradition of the church. His purpose is to emphasize that Jesus' Last Supper was held in connection with the Feast of the Passover. Hence the reference to the Feast of the Passover at the beginning. Hence too the statement at the conclusion of the entire episode, "And when they had sung a hymn, they went out to the Mount of Olives" (Mark 14:26; Matt. 26:30). The hymn referred to is the second part of the Passover-Hallel, namely, Psalms 114-118 (according to the Hillelites 115-118) which were sung at the conclusion of the Passover celebration. Thus there can be no doubt that according to the understanding of the evangelist we are to view the Last Supper of Jesus as a Passover meal—though one of a very special kind to be sure. In spite of this, research into the Gospels has been occupied for decades with the question whether Jesus' last meal was really a Passover or not. But if the Synoptic Gospels obviously and unambiguously refer to the Feast of Passover, why is there any question about the matter at all? Why has so much thought and effort been devoted to the problem?

The great difficulty, for which until now no final solution has yet been found, lies in the fact that the Synoptics on the one hand and the Gospel of John on the other presuppose a divergent chronology for the passion of Jesus. Having discussed the account of the Synoptics, we now inquire as to the time references of the Fourth Gospel. Although John does not report the institution of the Lord's Supper, he is certainly acquainted with the tradition of Jesus' Last Supper, for in chapter 13 he speaks of both the common meal and the identification of the traitor. According to John, however, these events could not have taken place on the day of the Passover. They must have occurred the evening of the preceding day, for the crucifixion itself occurred on the Day of Preparation. In fact, at the very hour when in the afternoon the paschal lambs were slain, Jesus dies as the true Paschal Lamb whose bones dare not be broken (John 19:36; cf. also John 18:28; 19:14). There is thus a difference of one full day between the chronology of the Synoptics and that of the Gospel of John. Is there any possibility of resolving this contradiction?

A number of efforts have been made to resolve the difficulty in terms of the hypothesis that the differences derive from the use of different calendars. Following the lead of earlier researchers,[7] the French scholar Annie Jaubert several years ago presented a sharply reasoned examination of this problem in which she offered a new suggestion for its solution,[8] one which has been greeted with approval by a number of scholars. Jaubert begins with the correct assertion that the community of true law-observers in Qumran on the banks of the Dead Sea lived by a calendar different from the one followed in Jerusalem. Whereas the priests of the temple oriented their calendar on the basis of the moon's orbit, the people of Qumran used a solar calendar which occasionally varied appreciably from the lunar calendar. According to the calendar dates used at Qumran the Jewish high holy days always occurred on the same day of the week. The Feast of the

---

[7] See Hermann L. Strack and Paul Billerbeck, *Kommentar zum Neuen Testament aus Talmud und Midrasch)* (Munich: Beck, 1926), II, 847 ff.

[8] See Annie Jaubert, *La Date de la Cène* (Paris: Gabalda, 1957).

Passover, for example, was always observed on a Wednesday. Since in Palestine, as is well known, the new day always begins with the evening before, Passover for the Qumran community must have started on a Tuesday evening after sundown. The official calendar used in Jerusalem, however, which was based on a lunar orbit, ordered matters differently. Here the only date given for Passover was the 14th of Nisan, with the particular day of the week varying from year to year.

Jaubert tries to draw upon this difference between the two Jewish calendars for a solution to the chronological problems in the story of the passion. She conjectures that Jesus lived not according to the official priestly calendar of Jerusalem but according to that of the community at Qumran. Since they celebrated the Feast of the Passover on Tuesday evening, it would follow that this was the time when Jesus ate that last meal with his disciples. Now all four evangelists agree that the day of crucifixion was followed by a sabbath, and that this was why the burial had to take place as quickly as possible, so that Jesus' body could still be buried before the day of rest began. Thus Jesus was crucified on a Friday. If he had celebrated the Passover with his disciples on a Tuesday, this would have left a time lapse of three days until his death on Friday. These considerations lead Jaubert to conclude that the Synoptists were right to place Jesus' Last Supper within the framework of a Passover Feast, but that they compressed the events of the three days into such rapid and brief succession as to give the impression that Jesus was crucified the very next day. She believes that John too, however, is correct in his chronology when he reports that Jesus died on the Day of Preparation for the Feast. In contrast to the Synoptists, John adhered not to the calendar of the Qumran community but to the official calendar of Jerusalem, and accordingly set the day of Jesus' death on the day before the Passover.

Though ingeniously conceived, this hypothesis is difficult

to credit.[9] In the first place, there is no evidence to support its underlying contention that the Synoptists have sharply abridged and compressed a series of events that happened on successive days. Above all, we would have to object that it is totally inconceivable that anyone in Jerusalem, where the paschal lambs had to be slaughtered at the temple, could be celebrating the Passover in accordance with the calendar of the heretics at Qumran. In Jerusalem it was possible to observe the feasts only on the basis of the official calendar established by the temple priesthood. Moreover, Jesus went to Jerusalem, not to Qumran; he obviously paid not the slightest attention to the problems of the calendar with which some Jewish factions were so greatly concerned. We must thus conclude that even a consideration of the calendar of the Qumran community will not clear up the problems connected with the chronology of Jesus' passion.

The contradictions between the Synoptists and John like-wise cannot be overcome by simply adhering to the one chronology and rejecting the other. On the contrary, what must be asserted is that neither the Synoptists nor John made their chronological statements because of any interest in his-torically accurate reporting. Even their references to the time intervals in the passion of Jesus represent theological affirm-ations; they serve the cause of proclamation. In Mark's ac-count the significance of the framework of events is perfectly clear. It is intended to show that the Supper of Jesus was connected with the paschal meal, and that it has now sup-planted that ancient Feast and become the festal celebration of all God's people, both Jews and Gentiles. Matthew follows Mark in this emphasis, and Luke underscores even more strongly than either of them the connection with the history of salvation. The redemption which God once effected for

9 For a critique of Jaubert's thesis see Josef Blinzler, "Qumran-Kalender und Passionschronologie," *Zeitschrift für die neutestamentliche Wissenschaft* 49 (1958), 238-251; Karl Georg Kuhn, "Zum essenischen Kalender," *Zeitschrift für die neutestamentliche Wissenschaft*, 52 (1961), 65-73; also the review of Jaubert's book by Joachim Jeremias in *The Journal of Theological Studies*, N.S., X, (1959), 131-133; and Jeremias, *The Eucharistic Words of Jesus, op. cit.*, pp. 24-25.

Israel in Egypt is set over against the redemption of the last time whereby God leads all his people everywhere out of bondage into freedom. John, however, wants to emphasize that Jesus dies at precisely the time when the paschal lambs are slaughtered. In I Corinthians 5:7 Paul says that "Christ, our paschal lamb, has been sacrificed." This ties in with a statement which Paul has taken over from the earliest Christian tradition. Christ is the Paschal Lamb of his church, and this is why the church now lives in a new aeon. The fourth evangelist takes up this thought and stresses that the death of Christ actually signifies the eschatological transition from old to new which brings to an end the cultus of Old Testament Judaism.

Inasmuch as all four evangelists shaped their accounts so largely with a view to Christian preaching and teaching, the question still persists whether Jesus' last meal was or was not a Passover meal. The answer is that this historical problem obviously cannot be solved on the basis of the introduction and framework with which the evangelists have circumscribed the eucharistic words of Jesus. The critical analysis must rather be restricted exclusively to the words themselves, which—as Paul indicates in I Corinthians 11—had been passed along during the first decades of the Christian church in the form of a separate and independent tradition. Is there anything in these few verses which would point to a Passover meal? Three aspects particularly must be considered and clarified in this respect.[10]

It must first be noted that Paul says Jesus partook of the meal "in the night in which he was betrayed." The Passover meal was also celebrated after the sun had set. Yet one cannot claim that this was the only occasion when an evening meal might be eaten. Mention of the evening hour, therefore, does not convincingly connect the Supper to the Feast of the Passover.

Equally inconclusive is the fact that at the Supper wine was consumed. It was a rule that in the course of the long

[10] See Jeremias, *The Eucharistic Words of Jesus, op. cit.,* pp. 41 ff.

Passover meal a cup of wine was to be passed to each participant several times, in fact, a total of four cups to all who were present for the celebration. The tradition tells us that Jesus, however, unlike John the Baptist, did not adhere to an ascetic way of life but occasionally drank a cup of wine. The annoyance on the part of those pious ones who disapproved of such behavior is attested by the derogatory way in which they referred to Jesus as a glutton and a drunkard (Matt. 11:19; Luke 7:34). Thus it is possible that Jesus and his disciples may have been drinking wine in connection with the Feast of the Passover, but they could equally well have been doing so for some other reason.

One might think that a parallel to the Feast of the Passover is to be found in the fact that it was customary to accompany the food and drink with words of interpetation. For in the course of the Passover liturgy celebrated in the home it was the head of the family who would explain the special customs that were observed on this particular day. The children would ask why bitter herbs and matzoth were to be eaten, and the father would answer that once upon a time the Egyptians had made bitter the captivity of the Israelites, and that because of the hastiness of their exodus from Egypt all that the Israelites were able to take with them for food along the way was bread that had not yet been leavened. The words of interpretation spoken during the Passover celebration thus refer to matters which distinguish this meal from all others eaten during the year. Moreover, these words are part of a liturgy. They are spoken at the beginning of the meal in order both to explain and to recall the significance of the Feast for the assembled fellowship of family and friends. Is there a connection, then, between the words spoken by Jesus concerning the bread and wine and this liturgical custom of explaining what is distinctive about the Feast of Passover?[11]

In two repects the words of Jesus differ greatly from the words spoken at the Passover, so greatly that a connection

[11] See Eduard Lohse, *Märtyrer und Gottesknecht* (Göttingen, 1955), p. 123.

between the two is very unlikely. In the first place, the words
of Jesus were spoken not as part of a liturgy that preceded
the meal but at the very moment when the bread was distributed and the cup was passed. Second, and more important,
Jesus' words are of a completely different kind. In the case
of the Passover the words explain the differences between
this particular meal and all others. The words of Jesus at the
Last Supper, on the contrary, deal not with bitter herbs and
matzoth but with bread and wine, that is, with such food and
drink as are used also upon other occasions.

We thus have to conclude that the words of institution do
not necessarily presuppose a connection with the Feast of the
Passover. With respect to the historical question we are not
able to discover anything beyond the fact that Jesus was
crucified in Jerusalem at about the time of the Passover. It
can no longer be determined whether that last meeting with
the disciples took place on the day of the Passover or shortly
before. To arrive at a correct exegesis of the words of institution themselves it is therefore of no importance whether
one subscribes to or denies the view that Jesus' last meal was
observed as part of the Passover celebration. The earliest
Christians—as Paul indicates in I Corinthians 11—apparently
did not consider it necessary to describe in detail the course
of Jesus' last meal. They were not interested in the details of
past events. Their sole interest lay in understanding the celebration of the Lord's Supper as a communion with Jesus
here and now. This is why these sentences are so obviously
liturgical in character, so brief and concise, even as we know
them from our own worship services. We ourselves quote
these words of institution in the liturgy of the Lord's Supper
without expressly mentioning their place within the larger
context of the passion story.

Just as it was of decisive importance for the earliest Christians to comprehend the contemporary significance of the
celebration and its proclamation of the Lord's death, so too
for us the most important task is to understand the meaning

of the statements "This is my body" and "This is my blood of the covenant, which is poured out for many" (Mark 14: 22-24; Matt. 26:26-28). For the explanation of these words we once again take as our starting point the terminology of the Gospel of Mark, which is repeated with only minor variations in Matthew. Luke, on the other hand, does not follow the text of Mark, but offers a differently worded version which is much closer to that of Paul. The similarities between Luke 22:15-19 and I Corinthians 11:23-26 do not derive from a literary dependence of Luke upon Paul such that Luke might have quoted from Paul's letter. They are better explained by the fact that both Paul and Luke used yet another tradition, one that must have been very early in origin and of a liturgical cast. For Paul assures us that he had first taken over these words and then delivered them to the Corinthians.

We are thus in possession of two different versions of the words of institution, both of which can be traced back to the very earliest period of the Christian church. This shows once again that the words of Jesus were not handed down in a time-hardened formulation as a venerable testimony to a past event but were rather delivered and proclaimed as the living words of Christ to his church. In contrast to the rabbis, who memorized word for word the sentences taught them by their teachers and who had to preserve the wording unchanged even to the slightest detail, the Christian church knows nothing of a law-imposed servitude to the letter. In the church it is the living voice of the gospel that is to be heard as the message of the truly present Lord. In order to answer the question as to which represents the earlier tradition, it will thus be necessary to compare the sentences quoted from Mark and Matthew with the formulations found in Paul and Luke.

When we turn our attention to the words spoken during the distribution of the bread, the first thing we notice is that Paul and Luke use a longer sentence: "This is my body which is (given) for you." In comparison with Mark 14:22 this represents an amplification whereby special emphasis is placed on the word "body."[12] It is the body of Christ given over unto death which establishes the bond of unity between all members in the one body of Christ. The reference here is thus to a connection between the celebration of the Lord's Supper and the church, a connection which the Corinthians had not sufficiently heeded and of which they must therefore again be made aware. In this instance the shorter version is surely the earlier one: "This is my body." It is spoken while the bread is being distributed and given to everyone sharing in the meal. The word is used to designate the gift being offered to all.[13] The body of Jesus Christ has been given unto death; in the common meal, therefore, all who partake are granted a share in the same body.

This inner meaning of the words of institution is expressed even more clearly in the second sentence. Before turning our attention to it, however, we must take note of the fact that Paul and Luke specifically add the command that this act be repeated within the circle of the disciples. The fact that this directive is not recorded in Mark and Matthew does not imply that there exists here a contradiction to the Pauline-Lucan version. For it is characteristic of liturgical phrases—and the words of institution are certainly to be so regarded—that they are repeated frequently, in fact, are intended for continual repetition, even though this is not always explicitly stated.

Beyond this we find in Paul and Luke another remark that is not found in Mark and Matthew. Prior to the words spoken over the cup there is the little phrase "after supper." This remark certainly stems from the earliest tradition and shows that the bread-word and the cup-word were originally

---

12 See Günther Bornkamm, "Herrenmahl und Kirche bei Paulus," *Zeitschrift für Theologie und Kirche*, 53 (1956), 335 ff.; reprinted in *Studien zu Antike und Urchristentum* (Munich: Kaiser, 1959), pp. 162 ff.
13 See Bornkamm, "Herrenmahl und Kirche bei Paulus," *Zeitschrift für Theologie und Kirche, op. cit.*, p. 329; and *Studien zu Antike und Urchristentum, op. cit.*, p. 156.

separated from one another by a period of eating and that both were thus part of a real meal. As the Lord's Supper gradually developed into a liturgical act and was no longer linked with an actual meal, the two words came into closer proximity and were bound together into a single act of worship. While in Mark the entire event has already been contracted into a single unit, the original division still exists in the case of Paul and Luke, who can thus be assumed in this respect to have preserved the earlier tradition.

Mark 14:24 and Matthew 26:28 record the words: "This is my blood of the covenant, which is poured out for many." The reference to blood is not necessarily to be viewed in relation to the blood of sacrificial animals, as though Jesus were being compared with the sacrifice of the Passover lamb. On the contrary, the Bible speaks of the shedding of blood even more often in connection with the offering of human life, beginning with the blood of Abel and on down to the blood of the prophets and witnesses. Thus this second sentence takes up what the first has already stated and emphasizes it even more clearly: the blood of Jesus has been shed, his life has been sacrificed "for many."

To speak of "all" in Aramaic or Hebrew it is necessary to say "many," inasmuch as in these languages no other word for "all" is available. Thus when in I Corinthians 10:17 Paul speaks about the Lord's Supper he translates the original word "many" into the Greek word "all": "Because there is one bread, we who are many are one body, for we all partake of the one bread." The expression "many" is therefore to be interpreted in the sense of the inclusive multiplicity spoken of, for example, in Isaiah 53:11-12 where we read that the Servant of God bears or has borne the sins of "many." As in the case of the earliest Christian confession in I Corinthians 15:3-5, so also in the words of institution reference is made to Isaiah 53 in order to reveal the inner meaning of Christ's death. He has become the substitute for all men by paying the price which they could not pay and by relieving them of the burden so that they might be free of it.

This statement about that blood poured out for many, though complete in itself, receives even more precise definition by means of the term "covenant," which is intended to characterize the new order of salvation established by Christ's death. The sacrifices that were once offered at Mount Sinai to confirm the bonds of the covenant had no power to expunge sins or atone for them (Exod. 24:3-8). The vicarious death of Christ by far surpasses them—and all the sacrifices of the old covenant. His death establishes the new order of salvation, that of the end time in which there is forgiveness of sins, life, and salvation. In terms of what is really involved it is altogether fitting that Matthew should add at the conclusion of the words of institution the phrase "for the forgiveness of sins" (Matt. 26:28).

In the version recorded by Paul and Luke the words "This is" are followed, not by "my blood of the covenant," but by "the new covenant in my blood." The concept of the covenant is here given even greater emphasis, although it is also stated that the covenant is established by the death of Christ. The designation of this covenant as "new" underscores the fact that it is the fulfillment of the prophet's words concerning the new covenant (Jer. 31:31 ff.). Therefore, in spite of the different formulations found in the two traditions of the words of institution, the one basic idea can again be seen. In the celebration of the Lord's Supper the assembled flock of the church experiences the present validity of the covenant established by Christ's death. It receives from its Lord the forgiveness of sins and knows itself to be constituted as the Lord's people to live a new life of faith and love.

Many of the problems which came to be of central concern in later Christian teaching were not problems for the earliest Christian churches. Since, as mentioned above, Luke recounts the episode involving the identification of the traitor only after he has described the institution of the Lord's Supper, the question has often been raised whether according to this Lucan version Judas was still around to participate in the Lord's Supper and thus might have received the bread and wine unworthily. At one time theologians of the Reformation tradition were busily occupied with the problem of the so-called *"manducatio impiorum,"* that is, the question whether those who come to the Table of the Lord unworthily really receive the body and blood of Christ—and thus eat it to their condemnation—or whether what is proffered to them is for them not at all the body and blood of Christ. As the New Testament, however, does not conceive of any change in the elements, any transubstantiation, neither does it display any special interest in the elements of the Lord's Supper as such, the bread/wine and body/blood. The very juxtaposition of body and covenant, as it exists in Paul and Luke, shows that the entire focus is on the act itself, on the enactment of the celebration. It is in this act though that the celebrating congregation knows itself to be in communion with its Lord.

Our critical analysis of the accounts of the Lord's Supper has shown that it is no longer possible to determine with exactness the historical course of the events connected with Jesus' last meal. Another important assertion though must be made at this point: Jesus' Last Supper with his disciples is part and parcel of that larger group of accounts, historically unimpeachable, which speak of the table fellowship which Jesus had not only with his disciples but above all with publicans and sinners. By coming to them, by eating and drinking with them, Jesus brought them the merciful nearness of God, the forgiveness of sins. It is this fellowship with the friend of publicans and sinners which the church maintains when, following Good Friday and Easter, in its celebrations of the Lord's Supper it professes its faith in the death and resurrection of Christ and receives anew the assurance of the forgiveness which it has through Christ, that forgiveness which is determinative of the new order of salvation. The church recalls the promise with which Jesus took leave of his flock, that he would drink the fruit of the vine over again with his own in the kingdom of God (Mark 14:25; Matt. 26:29; Luke 22:18) —which is why at the beginning of the Lord's Supper the church lifts her voice in prayer, saying: "Our Lord, come!" (I Cor. 16:22).

In their accounts the evangelists thus strive to emphasize both thoughts. First, the festal meal of the Christian church has its origin in that which happened once—indeed once-for-all—in the life of Jesus; it was instituted in the course of what happened then during his passion. Second, the church of the Lord stands between the aeons; it is on a pilgrimage, journeying toward the day when it will be united with its Lord and celebrate with him the messianic meal of joy.

4.

Gethsemane

The evangelist Mark effects a transition from the
account of the Last Supper to the next section by noting
that Jesus and his disciples sang a hymn and then went out
to the Mount of Olives. This once again presupposes that
Jesus left the overcrowded city in the evening with his disciples in order to spend the night outside the city walls. The
evangelist expands this brief remark by adding several words
spoken by Jesus to his disciples. They will all fall away, that
is, they will all lose faith. Even Peter, who gives passionate
assurance of his loyalty, will fall; this very night he will deny
his Lord. In this passage one can detect how depressing it
must have been for the church to recall not only that one
of the twelve was the betrayer but that all the disciples for-
sook Jesus and that even Peter denied him. In order to keep
the bitter offence of this failure on the part of all the disciples
from standing out even more prominently, the account
focusses not on the behavior of the disciples but on the
word of Jesus. He foresaw it all; he knew what must come
to pass. Though Peter might declare himself to be steadfast
and utterly reliable, Jesus still knows the hearts of men.
He knows how fickle men are and how quickly they forget
what they have just piously avowed (Mark 14:26-31).

Then there follows a more precise indication of the road
taken by Jesus and his disciples. They went to a place which
was called Gethsemane (Mark 14:32). This geographical
designation doubtless derives from an old tradition, for
where the evangelist was writing on his own he spoke only

in general terms of the Mount of Olives (vs. 26). According to John 18:1, Jesus spent this night in a garden on the other side of the Kidron Valley where he had often stayed with his disciples. The exact location of Gethsemane is not known. The earliest tradition shows no particular interest in the geographical location of the places where Jesus stayed. It focusses entirely on the portrait which the church was able to draw of its Lord in the act of confessing him.

Jesus instructs the disciples to sit while he goes to pray. He takes with him three of his disciples—Peter, James, and John—and begins to be distressed and troubled. The words of Jesus which the evangelist delivers to us are verses from the Old Testament. "Why are you cast down, O my soul?" asks the petitioner in Psalms 42:5, 11 and 43:5. And of Jonah it is said that he was sorrowful even unto death (Jonah 4:8). By having Jesus speak words from the Psalms it is suggested that his tribulation can be understood only in the light of the Scriptures, and overcome only in prayer. After going a little farther, beyond his three intimate disciples, Jesus falls on his knees and calls upon God. At first his prayer is reported in indirect discourse: "that, if it were possible, the hour might pass from him" (Mark 14:35). Then there follows, once again in direct discourse, the petition: "Abba, Father, all things are possible to thee; remove this cup from me; yet not what I will, but what thou wilt" (vs. 36).

This prayer of Jesus expresses his submission to the will of God. There is no doubt that for God all things are possible, that he is able either to usher in the hour or to turn it aside. The question is rather as to precisely what the will of God is, for this alone can determine the way Jesus is to go. To show Jesus' intimate relationship to the Father, the term "Abba, Father" is chosen as the word of address. To be sure, the designation of God as father was not at all uncommon in the Judaism of that time. Numerous Jewish prayers begin with this address, though by means of an accompanying qualification they usually indicate that it is the father of Israel who is meant. "Our father, our king"—it is in this sense that every Jew knows the fatherly name of God, who as king of all the world is also the father of his people. In the prayer of Jesus, however, as well as in the prayers of the Christian church, God is not addressed as the father of his people but as "my father" and "our father" (cf. Rom. 8:15; Gal. 4:6). "Abba" is the intimate pet name with which the little child addresses its father. When in the hour of his most severe trial Jesus addresses God by this name, he is already expressing, in the very form of address, the fact that the child belongs to the father and is seeking his will. True, he asks that the bitter cup of suffering might pass away. But God's will alone is to be determinative: not what I will, but what thou wilt.

Only once does the evangelist with modest reserve thus report the content of Jesus' prayer. In verse 39 we are told simply that Jesus prayed a second time, and in verse 41 a third prayer is just briefly intimated. Praying three times was always considered an especially fervent form of supplication to God (cf. II Cor. 12:8). It is for this reason that reference is made here to the thrice repeated prayer of Christ, the content of which, however, is obviously always the same.

The behavior of the disciples stands in sharp contrast to the prayer of Jesus born out of deepest tribulation. They seem not to have comprehended the significance of this hour. They sleep, they let the hour slip by, and their eyes seem to be held shut as if closed by overpowering forces. Thus they desert their Lord and ignore his admonition to wait and watch.

Jesus turns reproachfully to Peter with the question whether he could not have watched at least for a little while. He then directs to the entire band of disciples the challenge, "Watch and pray that you may not enter into temptation; the spirit indeed is willing, but the flesh is weak" (Mark 14:38, Matt. 26:41; Luke 22:40). This logion was undoubtedly taken from the earliest Christian paraenesis and inserted into the story at this point. For it is certainly not integral to the specific situation in which Jesus and his disciples now find themselves. Indeed, it is directed rather to the entire church as a summons to an attitude of watchfulness and prayer. The mention of temptation did not refer originally to the weariness of the disciples which caused them to close their eyes and fall asleep. Even if they had remained wide awake they still would not thereby have stood up to the hour of temptation with which the passion of Jesus was about to confront them. The important thing is to watch and pray incessantly, so long as the church is here on earth confronting temptation. The temptation Christians are to overcome is here viewed, not as those inner doubts which may arise, but as the perils which will befall God's people during the terror of the last days.

Judaism too lived in the expectation that just before the final consummation extraordinary dangers and frightful terrors would again break in upon the faithful ones. These terrors would be instigated by the devil himself with a view to seducing even the believers and leading them into apostasy. These trials of the last days must be withstood, and the only people truly prepared are those who put on the armor of God and are ready to offer determined resistance. The Dead Sea scriptures of the Qumran community repeatedly speak of the battle situation into which the people of God will be thrust during the last days. In the so-called "War Scroll" that deals with the battle of the sons of light against the sons of darkness we read how God's combat troops move out to do battle against the powers of darkness and ultimately to conquer them. To overcome temptation God's warriors are armed with the weapons of watchfulness and prayer, faithful perseverance in the service of God's people, and constant supplication to the God of Israel.

Karl Georg Kuhn has correctly called attention to the fact that this logion about not entering into temptation must be interpreted in terms of a background which we have come to know more intimately through the discovery of the Qumran manuscripts.[1] This is true not only with respect

---

[1] Karl Georg Kuhn, "Jesus in Gethsemane," *Evangelische Theologie*, XII (1952-1953), 260-285.

to the first statement which calls for watching and praying in
order that the church will be able to withstand the onslaughts
of the devil and not succumb to him. It is true also of the
subsequent justification given for this admonition—"The
spirit indeed is willing, but the flesh is weak"—the terminology of which can be understood only in the light of its background in the kind of Jewish thinking that had developed
within the Qumran community.

Older exegetes occasionally used to wonder whether this
sentence perhaps suggested some influence from Pauline
theology on the evangelist Mark. After all, Paul frequently
speaks of the antithesis between the flesh and the Spirit which
oppose one another in bitter conflict. On closer investigation,
however, we find that in Paul the concepts of flesh and
Spirit are set over against one another in a way quite different from that of Mark 14:38. When Paul speaks about the
flesh, what he has in mind is the natural man who acts in
his own strength and is convinced that by his own effort he
can attain salvation—be it the Jew who trusts in the law
and believes that by fulfilling the demands of the law he
shall prove himself righteous or the Greek who seeks wisdom
in the belief that as a wise man he will be able to attain
perfect knowledge. Both Jew and Greek fail to see that the
flesh can never attain salvation, that on the contrary natural
man is held in a captivity from which he cannot set himself
free, and that as flesh he is sold—and therefore lost—to the
power of sin, the law, and death. The Spirit on the other
hand, for Paul, represents God's eschatological dealing with
us now at the present time in the church of Jesus Christ. As
the symbol of the new aeon, the Spirit gives us even now assurance of the coming consummation. Spirit and flesh struggle against one another. For while as flesh man wants to
stand on his own and be righteous before God, it is only
through the God-given Spirit that new life can arise. Man is
unable to free himself from the bondage of the flesh. Only
God's Spirit opens the door to freedom. It is this Spirit-flesh
antithesis which would have kept Paul from ever saying

that the Spirit is willing but the flesh weak. When Paul speaks of the Spirit-flesh antithesis, what he has in mind is that Spirit of God against which the flesh of man contends; and this flesh is not weak, but of such mighty power that no man can subdue it. Christ alone has vanquished it, and he gives us the victory.

The antithesis of flesh and spirit in Mark 14:38 is not understood in the sense of Paul. It can be explained only in terms of the kind of Jewish thinking which has so recently been illuminated through the discovery of the Qumran manuscripts. For the battle which the sons of light must wage is serious, not because it must be fought against the foe who sets upon us from without, but because it takes place on the battlefield of man's heart. Two spirits, the spirit of falsehood and the spirit of truth, contend with one another until God's own victory puts an end to the battle.

This struggle though takes place within man himself, so that it is up to each person to assume his own battle position on the side of the spirit of truth.[2] But how can man arrive at the right decision and remain victorious in the battle? He is well aware of his own weakness and frailty. He knows that he is flesh, that he belongs to the evil flesh, and is bound to fall because of the sin of the flesh.[3] This is why man is in need of God's help. And this is also why the faithful must repeatedly be admonished and urged to be watchful and ever ready for battle, so that during the universal struggle of the last days they will be able to stand fast at their post.

When Mark (14:38) speaks of the willing spirit which is so easily smothered by the weak flesh, he is thinking only of man's spirit, which desires to do God's will but is often prevented from realizing its intentions by man's own weakness and frailty. While Paul would have said the flesh is so strong that it irresistably thwarts all good intentions, we read in Mark that the flesh is weak and that man consequently is not in a position to perform what he knows in his

[2] Manual of Discipline 4: 23-25.
[3] Cf. Manual of Discipline 11: 9 ff.

spirit to be right. These ideas, stemming from the Jewish tradition, have been taken over into the Christian paraenesis in order to enjoin Christians to remain steadfast during the tribulations of the last days and to watch and pray so that Satan with his crafty assaults can make no perilous inroads.

In placing these words within the context of the Gethsemane story the evangelist applies to the sleeping disciples this summons to watch and pray. The disciples are a good example of how easily men can let an opportunity slip by and how quickly they can succumb to temptation. By means of this admonition directed to all Christians the message of the Gethsemane story is at once made to transcend the specific historical situation; it becomes a word addressed to the churches of all times and places. The summons becomes the more urgent as, despite his enjoinder, the very disciples who are closest to Jesus fail to remain awake, and in their drowsiness are unable to persevere even for a little while.

Three times the process is repeated—Jesus wrestles all alone in prayer while the disciples fall fast asleep. When Jesus returns for the third time and again finds them asleep, he tells them it is now too late. The opportunity has been irretrievably lost. The moment for proving their steadfastness is gone. The hour has come in which the Son of man must be delivered into the hands of sinners. The word "sinners" here refers to the Gentiles who, according to the Jewish view, were one and all sinners because they did not have the divine law and were thus ignorant of God's will and could not help but sin. The Son of man is surrendered into the hands of the Gentiles—the contrast could not have been more sharply put. He who bears the title indicative of messianic fulfillment is thrust out into uttermost desolation, abandoned by his people, and given over to the heathen. The concluding sentence, "Rise, let us be going; see, my betrayer is at hand" (Mark 14:42), serves as a transition to the following story that deals with the arrest of Jesus.

Viewed in retrospect, it can be seen that what we have in this story of the temptation of Jesus and of his wrestling in prayer is an earlier tradition to which certain details have been added. At first we are told that Jesus goes to Gethsemane with his disciples; then we are told that he takes Peter, James, and John along. The content of Jesus' prayer is repeated twice, but there is the implication of its having been repeated three times. In each instance the disciples sleep on unknowingly. With Karl Georg Kuhn,[4] we might raise the question whether the evangelist here interwove accounts from two different sources and whether the repetition can be traced back to his manner of reproducing each detail of the story, first according to the one version and then according to the other. The attempt to separate the materials into two different strands, however, does not produce a convincing explanation. For it can be shown that the repetition does not derive from a confluence of two different streams of narrative but from an amplification of one originally brief version of the Gethsemane tradition.

In the first place, Luke's account reveals that even after the Gospel of Mark had been written further additions were still made. After Jesus had prayed the first time—thus writes Luke—an angel from heaven appeared in order to strengthen him in his agonizing prayer struggle (Luke 22:43-44). This legendary elaboration was undoubtedly a later addition.

At several points though the Marcan version itself discloses that later amplifications must have taken place. The fact that the Lord took with him only his three intimate disciples can surely be traced back to the evangelist himself. For the Gospel of Mark speaks more than once of how these three disciples were singled out for some unusual experience or special instruction. They are witnesses to the raising of Jairus' daughter (Mark 5:37); to them it is granted to behold the transfiguration of Jesus (Mark 9:2); and it is to them that Jesus speaks about what is to happen in the last days (Mark 13:3). Again, when one compares the two verses which cite the content of Jesus' prayer, it is unmistakably clear that the prayer presented in the form of direct discourse

4 See Karl Georg Kuhn, *op. cit.*, pp. 263 ff., esp. n. 25.

(Mark 14:36) is more recent than the petition recounted in the form of indirect discourse (vs. 35). We shall also have to assess as a later elaboration the mention of Jesus' prayer being repeated three times, especially since no change in content is connected with the repetition. We have already shown conclusively that a logion from the paraenesis of the church was used in verse 38. Finally, at the end of the story, there is an expanded and elaborated finale in the phrase concerning the suffering Son of man (vs. 41b) and in the subsequent summons to rise and go (vs. 42). If these verses are thus individually and critically analyzed, we find that there remains only a very brief original tradition involving the prayer of Jesus in the hour of tribulation before he sets out on the way to the cross. Is it possible to trace this tradition back to a historical root?

It is not difficult, of course, to imagine that in anticipation of the suffering that awaited him Jesus should have been greatly distressed and troubled and that he should have wrestled in prayer for strength to withstand the trials. In critically analyzing the Gethsemane tradition, however, it will be necessary at the outset to keep in mind that this story was not a part of the earliest account of the passion, which actually began—as we have already seen—with the arrest of Jesus. Furthermore, it must be remembered that there were no eyewitnesses to give a firsthand report on that hour Jesus spent in prayer. Even the early church was concerned with this question. Its proposed answer was that later on the risen Lord may have told his disciples exactly what transpired there at Gethsemane. On the other hand, a number of exegetes have contended that the Gethsemane story can be traced back to the Petrine tradition; for neither the drowsiness which did not immediately and necessarily turn to full sleep nor the distance which separated them from the praying Jesus would of necessity have prevented the disciples from hearing some of the words he spoke in his anguished prayer.[5]

5 See Friedrich Hauck, *Das Evangelium des Markus* (Leipzig: Deichert, 1931), p. 172.

One could hardly insist, though, that such a conjecture represents a convincing explanation.

We come closer to an answer to this question when we compare the tradition employed here by the evangelist with the words used in the Letter to the Hebrews, where we read that in the days of his flesh Jesus offered up prayers and supplications, with loud cries and tears, to him who was able to save him from death, and that he was heard for his godly fear (Heb. 5:7).[6] It is true that these words from the Letter to the Hebrews pose several problems that are not easily solved, for example, whether Jesus was really "heard" or whether it is not more correct to say that his petition was rejected. With respect to our immediate investigation the main point that must be kept in mind is that Hebrews 5:7 witnesses to a primitive Christian tradition which speaks of the prayer of Jesus in the hour of tribulation. This tradition of course is not necessarily associated with the story of the passion; the Letter to the Hebrews speaks of "the days of his flesh" generally. But since it was customary among the earliest Christians to seek to interpret and understand everything that had to do with the earthly sojourn of Jesus in the light of the Scriptures, the prayer which in his distress he addressed to God was also viewed in the light of the Psalms and was expressed in their terminology. For the church was familiar with how in the Psalms the suffering suppliant in his distress and desolation cries out to God and in prayer comes to know the will of God and to find comfort and strength for accepting and following the way that is set before him. Hence in speaking of Jesus' prayer in his hour of tribulation it could use words of the Psalms in which the petitioner cries out in extreme anguish and tribulation.

In the Gospel of John too there is evidence to suggest that the tradition incorporated in the Gethsemane episode could not have been unknown to the evangelist. This evidence is

[6] See Martin Dibelius, "Gethsemane", trans. Morton S. Enslin in *The Crozer Quarterly*, XII, No. 3 (July, 1935), 254-265; and Dibelius, *From Tradition to Gospel, op. cit.*, pp. 211-213.

found not in the passion narrative itself, which does not begin until chapter 18 with the arrest of Jesus, but in an earlier section. After the account of the anointing and the entry of Jesus into Jerusalem at the beginning of chapter 12, it is reported that some Greeks had come because they wanted to see Jesus (12:20 ff.). To this episode the evangelist appended several dominical sayings, derived from the common Christian tradition, about following and about the path of suffering which the disciples would have to walk with Jesus. And then comes the passage in John 12:27-28: " 'Now is my soul troubled. And what shall I say? "Father, save me from this hour"? No, for this purpose I have come to this hour. Father, glorify thy name.' Then a voice came from heaven, 'I have glorified it, and I will glorify it again.' " The crowd standing by does not understand what is happening, but thinks that it had thundered. The fourth evangelist frequently gives special emphasis to this attitude of patent misunderstanding in order to demonstrate the blindness of unbelief. It can also be deduced from the very terminology of these verses that they reflect the evangelist's own way of speaking. It is characteristic of him to emphasize the word "glorify." For the glorification of Jesus is linked inseparably with his suffering. The glory of God, which believers can discern in the incarnate One, is made manifest precisely in his humiliation, in his journey to the cross. If one sets aside this Johannine formulation of the sentences, what remains is a brief tradition which speaks of the tribulation of Jesus in anticipation of the impending suffering and of his prayer to be saved from this hour. Thus the Gospel of John, like the Letter to the Hebrews, testifies to the fact that the earliest Christian tradition regarded Jesus as a man of prayer who by looking up to God stands fast in his most difficult hour. There are no scruples about portraying Jesus as a person who was troubled and oppressed by the approaching danger. For the Christ whom the church confesses was tempted in all things—but he withstood the temptation and by his victory obtained salvation for us.

It was this understanding of the tribulation and suffering of Jesus which was decisive in the development of the Gethsemane story, whose content therefore cannot be traced back to a historical report but is directly connected with the earliest Christology. It is this Christology which in words derived from Scripture is given verbal expression—and in the Gethsemane episode a pictorial form. The logion involving the prayer for the removal of the tribulation, drawn as it is from the paraenesis of the early church, helps to strengthen the significance of the Gethsemane episode, even as the embellishment involving three separate prayers was supposed to make even more indelible the impact of the story. Finally, the concluding words connect the episode with the course of the entire passion narrative: the hour is come; the Son of man is delivered up. Thus this pericope shows us how the early church originally viewed and interpreted the passion: the Son of man is thrust into the uttermost desolation, seized by tribulation and distress. The dereliction of Jesus Christ, however, takes place in accordance with God's inscrutable will, which Jesus comes to know in prayer and to which he obediently submits.

The captors now appear on the scene. Led by Judas, they have been sent out by the Jewish authorities to arrest Jesus and take him into custody. With these sentences the evangelist now picks up the thread of the earliest account of the passion which in quick sequence tells of Jesus' arrest, the proceeding before the Sanhedrin, his sentencing by the Roman governor, and his crucifixion and death. The Gospel of John too reports that Jesus was arrested in the garden beyond the Kidron Valley by the soldiers who had been sent out to apprehend him. By suggesting that in addition to the Jews who had come with Judas there were also Roman soldiers (John 18:3), the fourth evangelist goes beyond the Synoptists. His account raises the question as to who it actually was that instigated the action against Jesus. According to John we must assume at least some participation on the part of the Roman occupying powers. Yet according to the Synoptic account the Jewish authorities alone were responsible for the measures taken against Jesus. The fact is, as we hope to show yet in greater detail, that the Synoptic account is historically the correct one. After all, it is entirely understandable that the Jewish authorities should look upon the preaching and activity of Jesus as an attack directed against the law and the cult. Undoubtedly the cleansing of the temple together with Jesus' warning of impending judgment had to be accepted as a challenge which might seriously have jeopardized the position and standing of the temple's governing priesthood.

The story of the arrest is told in a few words. Judas is introduced as one of the twelve, as if the reader did not yet know who he was. Again we see that what originally began at this point was an early account involving no prior reference to previously narrated events. The appointed sign is the kiss, the greeting of respect with which pupils were accustomed to meet their rabbis. It is used to show the soldiers whom they are to seize. They lay hands on Jesus and arrest him (Mark 14:43-46; Matt. 26:47-50; Luke 22:47-48; John 18:2 ff.).

In the course of transmission this very brief account was made more vivid through elaboration. In the first place, Mark mentions a slave of the high priest whose ear is cut off by one of Jesus' disciples (Mark 14:47). The description given by the other Gospel writers demonstrates how the tradition continues to expand in legendary fashion. Luke is able to say that it was the slave's right ear (Luke 22:50). Matthew and Luke cite a command of Jesus in which he admonishes his disciple to sheathe his sword, and Matthew goes on to cite a word of Jesus to the effect that all who take the sword will perish by the sword (Matt. 26:52; Luke 22:51). Luke adds the touching line about Jesus healing the ear of the slave. Finally, John goes so far as to supply us with the name of the slave. It was Malchus, and the disciple who wounded him was Peter (John 18:10).

With a few words Jesus addresses himself to the captors. They have come against him in secret as if they were going to seize a robber, though they could well have found him at any time when he was teaching publicly in the temple. This statement expresses the indignation aroused by the manner in which the authorities had proceeded, an indignation which the early Christians had harbored with respect to the Jews. Yet they know too that the Scriptures must be fulfilled (Mark 14:49). Things must come to pass in this manner for the Servant of God is to be abandoned to utter desolation, mistreated, and reckoned with the transgressors. Thus Jesus is brought before the Jewish authorities for trial and judgment, while his disciples all forsake him and flee (Mark 14:50).

5.

The Trial

Immediately after his arrest Jesus is brought before the high priest, who promptly assembles the chief priests, the elders, and the scribes (Mark 14:53). This hastily called meeting of the Sanhedrin was supposed to provide a legal justification for the death sentence that long ago had been pronounced against Jesus. However, it was difficult to find for such a sentence any legal ground that might have the slightest semblance of validity (Mark 14:55). When the testimony of the called witnesses fails to accomplish this purpose, the high priest approaches Jesus and addresses to him the decisive question whether he is the Christ, the Son of the Blessed (Mark 14:61). When Jesus answers in the affirmative and substantiates his answer by reference to two Scripture passages (Ps. 110:1; Dan. 7:13), the high priest in horror tears his mantle and charges the members of the Sanhedrin to pass judgment in the light of the blasphemy that has just been heard. Thereupon they all condemn Jesus as deserving of death. Thus at the conclusion of the interrogation the Sanhedrin hands down a unanimous verdict of guilty and condemns Jesus to death.

After the proceeding is over Jesus is mocked and ridiculed. They cover his face and challenge him to prophesy. This picture of the despised and humiliated Lord bears the features of the Old Testament portrayal of the suffering Servant of God (Isa. 50:6). Just as in those days no credence was given to the word of the prophet, just as the Servant gave his back to the smiters and his cheeks to those who pulled out the beard and did not hide his face from shame and spitting, so Jesus too is covered with scorn and spittle and given over to contempt and suffering (Mark 14:65).

In its essential features this story is certainly based on the tradition then available to the evangelist Mark. He has given a new form to the story, however, by linking it closely with the episode of Peter's denial. Already in the introduction mention is made of Peter, who after the arrest had followed Jesus at a cautious distance and then ventured right into the courtyard of the high priest where the guards had started a fire to keep themselves warm during the cold night (Mark 14:53-54). At this point nothing more is said about Peter while the proceeding before the Sanhedrin is reported. Only after the report of the trial is the account of Peter's conduct again resumed and brought to its conclusion. The result is an impressive contrast. While Jesus publicly confesses before the Sanhedrin itself that he is the Messiah and Son of God, his disciple refuses even before the maid and servants of the high priest to make the confession of loyalty demanded of him, and by this denial he renounces his relationship to his Lord. Matthew has retained this type of narrative approach —used by Mark in other instances as well (cf., e.g., Mark 5:21-43)—whereby through combining closely two stories the significance of each is enhanced. Luke, on the other hand, seeks to effect a clearer and more intelligible order of events and has thus severed the connection between the two stories, reporting first the denial by Peter and then the proceeding before the Sanhedrin (Luke 22:54-71).

Jesus' trial before the Sanhedrin was referred to already in the three passion predictions to which we gave our attention on pages 11-14. While the first of these predictions (Mark 8:31, Matt. 16:21; Luke 9:22) merely says that the Son of man will be rejected by the elders, the chief priests, and the scribes, and then rise again after three days, the brief summary of the passion set forth in Mark 10:33-34 (cf. Matt. 20:18-19; Luke 18:31-33) goes into greater detail: "Behold, we are going up to Jerusalem; and the Son of man will be delivered to the chief priests and the scribes, and they will condemn him to death, and deliver him to the Gentiles; and they will mock him, and spit upon him, and scourge him, and kill him; and after three days he will rise." These statements, which the evangelist formulated in reliance upon the earliest Christian tradition, involve a difficult problem. For we read first of all that the Son of man will be given into the hands of the Jewish authorities and that they will condemn him to death. But then it is announced that Jesus will be delivered to the Gentiles, that they will mock and ridicule him, and finally nail him to the cross. This means that it was not only before the Jewish Sanhedrin that a trial was conducted which concluded with Jesus' conviction but that the Roman occupation powers also passed sentence upon him and immediately thereafter carried out the execution. Thus already in the pre-Marcan tradition there is mention of two separate trials, one following shortly after the other, one before the highest Jewish tribunal, the other before the governor Pontius Pilate.

What is the relationship between these two statements, according to which Jesus was sentenced twice in succession by two entirely different tribunals? To answer this question we must first examine carefully the Gospel accounts of the trial of Jesus.[1] While Matthew adheres rigidly to Mark's sequence of events, Luke conspicuously departs from this version at a number of points. Luke has not only placed the story of Peter's denial first, prior to the hearing before the high priest, but he has also condensed to the utmost his account of the proceeding. He has omitted the testimony of the witnesses who spoke about Jesus' words concerning the temple and has focussed the interrogation exclusively on the critical question asked by the high priest: "If you are the Christ, tell us" (Luke 22:67). In response to this question Jesus acknowledges that he is the Son of man. Asked again whether he is the Son of God, he answers, "You say that I am." What fol-

---

[1] See Eduard Lohse, "Der Prozess Jesu Christi," in *Ecclesia und Res publica. Festschrift für K. D. Schmidt* (Göttingen, 1961), pp. 24-89.

lows then, according to Luke, is, not a death sentence pronounced by the Sanhedrin, but simply a determination that
no further testimony is needed since they have heard it from
his own lips (Luke 22:71). According to Luke, therefore,
Jesus was indeed questioned before the Sanhedrin in a hearing which was supposed to reveal and determine his guilt,
but the death sentence was actually pronounced by Pilate
alone, before whose judgment seat the question of life and
death for the accused was argued and decided.

At this point the question arises whether this Lucan version is to be traced back to another source, a source independent of Mark. Our analysis of the account of the Lord's Supper has already demonstrated that we must indeed reckon
with the possibility that in several sections of his story of
the passion Luke may well have been dependent upon a
source other than that of Mark's Gospel. It is difficult to determine, however, the exact extent and scope of this special
source, or whether the occasional discrepancies derive from
the use here and there of independently transmitted fragments of tradition.[2] At any rate, it will be necessary carefully
to consider this question in connection with each separate
pericope of the passion narrative.

What then is the situation with respect to the Lucan account of the trial of Jesus? In a comprehensive monograph
Paul Winter has recently propounded the view that in his
account of Jesus' trial Luke made use of a second source different from the Gospel of Mark.[3] In support of his contention
Winter points to the fact that already in Jesus' third passion
prediction there is no mention whatever of the Sanhedrin's
being involved in the trial. Instead it is stated only that "we
are going up to Jerusalem, and everything that is written
of the Son of man by the prophets will be accomplished. For
he will be delivered to the Gentiles, and will be mocked and
shamefully treated and spit upon; they will scourge him and

---

[2] See p. 40 above.
[3] See Paul Winter, *On the Trial of Jesus* (Berlin: De Gruyter, 1961), pp.
27-28.

kill him, and on the third day he will rise" (Luke 18:31-33).
While Luke is undoubtedly dependent upon Mark at this
point, he has deliberately altered the content of the passage.
In contrast to Mark he strives to emphasize the idea that in
the passion of Jesus all the words of the prophets were fulfilled, and for this reason refers to all those things that were
written of the Son of man by the prophets. As in the Easter
stories Luke repeatedly points out that the promises of the
Old Testament from Moses to all the prophets and the
Psalms have been fulfilled (cf. Luke 24:25-27, 44), so here
in connection with the passion of Jesus he is also intent on
directing special attention to the words of prophecy. He
therefore lays special stress on this motif in the third passion
prediction by limiting his enumeration of the events of the
passion to the handing over of Jesus to the Gentiles and his
execution at their hands, together of course with the reference to the fulfillment of the Scriptures.

The same process is repeated in connection with Luke's
account of the trial of Jesus. Here too it can be shown that
he not only relies on Mark's version but has also altered it
by abbreviating it. In the Marcan version the crucial word
that Jesus speaks to the high priest is as follows: "I am; and
you will see the Son of man sitting at the right hand of
Power, and coming with the clouds of heaven" (Mark
14:62). Whereas in Mark the juxtaposition of Psalm 110:1
and Daniel 7:13 calls pointed attention to the messianic
dignity of Jesus and to the majesty of the Lord at the Parousia, in the case of Luke the expectation of the imminent
return of the Lord has receded far into the background and
lost considerably in importance. As in general it is characteristic of Luke's theology that eschatology is removed from
the center to the periphery, so here too the passage from the
Marcan model has been changed and reduced to the statement: "But from now on the Son of man shall be seated at
the right hand of the power of God" (Luke 22:69). The
juxtaposition of the two Old Testament passages can still
be discerned, but the reference to the Parousia has been

omitted. This comparison of the same verse in both Mark and Luke helps us to see clearly that the Lucan version is in any case the later of the two.

What does the writer of the Fourth Gospel have to tell us about the proceeding against Jesus and about his sentencing? The sequence of events in John's Gospel differs in its details from that found in the Synoptics. After his arrest (John 18:1-11), Jesus is first brought before Annas, father-in-law of the currently ruling high priest Caiaphas, who interrogates him and sends him on to Caiaphas (John 18:12-24). We are not told whether the members of the Sanhedrin were present. In the palace of the high priest Peter denies his Lord (John 18:25-27). Caiaphas has Jesus taken to the praetorium where the governor conducts the interrogation and passes sentence (John 18:28 ff.). The Johannine version is thus completely independent of the Synoptics—even though it was undoubtedly written subsequent to these—since, as can be seen in the dialogues between Jesus and Annas and between Jesus and Pilate, in large measure it has been shaped by the theology of the fourth evangelist. This critical analysis of the description of the trial of Jesus in all Four Gospels leads us to the conclusion that the earliest version is found in the Gospel of Mark and that consequently this Gospel must serve as the basis for our discussion of the problems connected with that trial.

The agreement of all four evangelists that the execution of Jesus was carried out at the command of the Roman governor accords fully with the statement in John 18:31 in which the Jews say to Pontius Pilate, "It is not lawful for us to put any man to death." Since capital punishment was forbidden to the Jews, and since supreme legal authority had been vested in the governor, capital cases had to be tried by him and it was he who had to pass judgment. In recent discussions it has occasionally been held that this statement in the Gospel of John is not historically accurate. Following the research of Jean Juster,[4] Hans Lietzmann in

4 Jean Juster, *Les Juifs dans l'empire Romain* (Paris, 1914).

a brief and penetrating treatise concerning the trial of Jesus
has maintained that even under Roman rule the Jews continued to hold jurisdiction in capital cases. They themselves
were therefore fully empowered to condemn and execute
a criminal. For this reason alone the Marcan version of
Jesus' trial, which speaks of a Roman verdict being delivered and executed, must be historically incorrect.[5] In the
course of the theological discussion some scholars have vigor-
ously opposed Lietzmann's thesis while others have agreed
with it; to this day it still claims a number of supporters.
The most recent scholar to espouse and advance Leitzmann's
critical view is Paul Winter,[6] who tends to reject outright
the possibility that the Jews had any part in the trial of
Jesus. According to Winter, Jesus was in the final analysis
nothing but a Jew, akin in most respects to the Pharisees.
Although he espoused a number of distinct views, Jesus
nevertheless remained a faithful son of his people. It was
because of the popular movement incited by him that he
became politically suspect to the Roman governor, who
then had his soldiers arrest him. The high priest had no
alternative but to yield to the Roman pressure and surrender Jesus—in order to avoid even worse things. In Winter's view, Jesus is thus made to appear as the prototype
of the Jew who in this world is always persecuted and condemned to indescribable suffering.

Now such conclusions undoubtedly go far beyond what
can be substantiated on the basis of the data recorded in
the Gospels. Before we can examine critically the assump-
tions on which this conception of Jesus' trial is based, however, it is necessary to clarify first the question raised anew
by Lietzmann concerning the juridical situation existing in
Palestine at that time.[7] The Sanhedrin, whose origin prob-

---

[5] Hans Lietzmann, *Der Prozess Jesu* (Berlin, 1931); reprinted in *Kleine
Schriften II: Studien zum Neuen Testament,* ed. Kurt Aland (Berlin:
Akademie, 1958), pp. 251-263.

[6] See Paul Winter, *op. cit.*

[7] See Eduard Lohse, "Synedrion," in *Theologisches Wörterbuch zum
Neuen Testament, op. cit.,* VII, 858 ff.

ably goes back to the time of Persian rule in Palestine, was a senate of aristocrats which constituted the highest Jewish governing body. It consisted of three groups—the chief priests, the elders, and the scribes. At its meetings the high priest presided. The rights and powers of the Sanhedrin had already been severely curtailed during the rule of the Hasmonean princes, and further restrictions had been sustained under the rule of Herod (37-4 B.C.). Because it had once dared to call the young Herod to account for the death sentences he had arbitrarily carried out in Galilee, the king later took bloody revenge. Many of the council members who had once placed him under their jurisdiction were now killed at Herod's command and replaced by compliant persons willing to take direction from the king. Though the legal competency of the Sanhedrin was not altogether suspended, in actuality the king administered justice on his own, without giving heed to the Sanhedrin or allowing it to participate in judicial determinations. Herod ruled alone in the land as king and judge, refusing to limit his power in any way out of consideration for the Sanhedrin.

When Judea came under the administration of Roman procurators after 6 B.C., the Sanhedrin was again able in modest measure to play a role in local affairs. The Roman governor resided in Caesarea by the sea. He came up to Jerusalem only during the Jewish high holy days, to be able to observe things for himself and keep a watchful eye on what the people were doing. The Jewish authorities in the holy city had the right to render judgment in all matters pertaining to the Jewish cult and congregation and to punish offences committed against the law provided these were not capital offenses. Beyond this, the Sanhedrin had been granted power by the Romans to punish even with death any Gentile—even any Roman—who trespassed the bounds of the temple and entered the holy area. The granting of this special privilege, however, certainly cannot be taken to mean that even under the rule of the Roman governor the Jewish Sanhedrin still maintained jurisdiction in capital cases.

Those scholars who claim that even under Roman rule the Jews were able to inflict capital punishment have based their views primarily on reports that even during the years 6-70 A.D. executions took place on order of the Jewish authorities. In this connection the following instances are cited.

1. The daughter of a priest was executed by burning for having committed a carnal act. This incident recorded in the Mishna[8] probably took place, however, during the years 41-44 A.D., when under the rule of King Herod Agrippa I the Jews once again for a brief time had a political existence of their own in which Jewish law alone was the guide and rule.

2. In Acts 12:2 mention is made of the death of James, son of Zebedee and brother of John. His execution, however, most certainly also took place during this time of King Herod Agrippa I.

3. Later on, after the death of the Governor Porcius Festus when a successor had not yet been named, the high priest Ananus used this opportune interval to have James the brother of the Lord tried quickly, sentenced by the Sanhedrin, and then stoned to death.[9] Because he had proceeded on his own in this matter and overstepped the authority granted him by the Romans, he was later called to account by them and deposed from office.

4. Finally, the stoning of Stephen reported in Acts 7:54—8:3 is mentioned. Yet his execution can hardly be regarded as the result of an orderly judicial process. It is rather a lynching perpetrated by an enraged mob.

It is true that now and then the Romans in this case or that may have allowed the Jews to have their way, not interfering even though they transgressed the limits set for them. An incident of this kind, however, can never be construed

8 Sanhedrin 7:2.
9 Josephus *Antiquities* xx. 9, 1.

to represent the rule rather than the exception. Even though the Jews for their part had never renounced their right by authority of the divine law to inflict capital punishment, they were nevertheless prevented from freely exercising that right as long as they were subject to the rule of Rome. This juridical situation is reflected in the later reports of the talmudic tradition from which we learn that forty years prior to the destruction of the temple the Jews had been deprived of the right to conduct trials involving capital charges.[10] In this connection the number "forty" is not to be taken literally; this round number is undoubtedly intended simply to date the beginning of Roman suzerainty over Judea.

This conclusion to which our deliberations have brought us is in keeping with the practice followed by the Romans in other provinces as well, where they permitted the local authorities to continue and to regulate all matters involving the local inhabitants. Supreme legal authority, however, was vested in the governor, before whose tribunal all Roman citizens too were accountable. Capital cases were tried by the governor, who in addition was able at all times and at his own discretion to intervene in any other current court proceedings.[11] Since the line of demarcation between the competency of the local authorities and that of the governor were obviously not always clearly defined, any ambiguity or confusion that might arise could only offer the Romans a welcome opportunity to intervene, especially where they deemed it expedient to take jurisdiction themselves. Presumably in Judea too the range of the powers granted to the Sanhedrin had not been determined in detail; hence the governor was always in a position to impose incontestable sentences. During the high holy days, while the governor was in residence within the walls of Jerusalem, the Sanhedrin would certainly have been unable to try a capital case and to carry out the

10 See the instances cited in Strack and Billerbeck, *op. cit.*, (Munich: Beck, 1922), I, 1026-1027.
11 See A. N. Sherwin-White, *Roman Society and Roman Law in the New Testament* (Oxford: Clarendon, 1963), pp. 1-47.

verdict without having the governor interpret such an action as a challenge to his own authority. Therefore the statement in John 18:31 accords in fact with the legal situation that existed at that time: the Jews were not permitted to impose and execute the death sentence.

The Gospels' statement that the Sanhedrin delivered Jesus over to the governor so that he might pronounce the death sentence is fully in accord with the situation as it existed in the Palestine of Jesus' day. If we compare the report of the proceeding before the Sanhedrin, however, with the legal statutes of the Jewish Halakah, we have to conclude that a number of grave violations were committed against the precepts of the law.

1. In the first place, the Mishna treatise Sanhedrin directs that capital cases be tried only during the day, not at night.[12] Yet the proceeding against Jesus was conducted at night.

2. The verdict is never to be pronounced on the first day of the proceeding; there must be at least a second session, held the next day, at which the final determination of the verdict can be made.[13] In the case of Jesus, however, the verdict against him was pronounced during the very first session of the trial.

3. Court proceedings were not to be conducted on the sabbath or on holy days, in fact, not even on Days of Preparation, lest the commandment concerning the day of rest be broken.[14] This precept was clearly violated, for the Sanhedrin assembled during the night of the Passover to try the case against Jesus.

4. According to Sanhedrin 7:5 it is considered blasphemy to utter the name of Yahweh, a word which the Jews reverently avoided lest they offend against the divine honor and desecrate it. Jesus, however, did not speak that name at all; in the sight of the Mishna therefore he could not have said anything that might have been adjudged as blasphemy.

12 Sanhedrin 4:1.
13 *Ibid.*
14 *Ibid.*

5. Finally, it must be pointed out that the official place of assembly was in the temple area, in the so-called "hall of hewn stone." On the eve of the Feast, however, it must certainly have been impossible to assemble there since the gates of the temple were kept locked at night. The Synoptists leave us with the impression that the Sanhedrin assembled in the palace of the high priest and there carried on the proceeding against Jesus. Since there is no mention anywhere else of a session ever being held in the house of the high priest, the procedure as described by the evangelists deviates at this point too from customary practice.

In order to evaluate these contradictions correctly it must be remembered that the legal statutes codified in the Mishna reflect the views of those rabbis who inclined toward Pharisaism, who after the destruction of Jerusalem in 70 A.D. assumed sole leadership of Judaism and determined the development of the legal tradition. Before 70 A.D., however, the Sanhedrin did not proceed along lines laid down by the Pharisees, for at that time its decisions were determined by the Sadducean majority. In his study of the trial of Jesus, Josef Blinzler has correctly and emphatically called attention to this important difference.[15] Although we know but little of the details of the Sadducean legal statutes, we can at least say this much in general, that unlike the Pharisees the Sadducees consistently followed the older tradition and stood for a stricter interpretation of the directives found in the law. The Pharisees tended to interpret these statutes more leniently, and after the destruction of Jerusalem they managed to win general acceptance for their views. Blinzler thus attempts to attribute the contradictions between the events as reported in the Gospels and the precepts of the Mishna to the fact that the Mishna was shaped by the teachings of the Pharisees, while the statutes of the Sadducees need not necessarily have been in conflict with the procedures employed

---

[15] See Josef Blinzler, *Der Prozess Jesu* (3d ed.; Regensburg: Pustet, 1960), pp. 154-163. [Cf. *idem, The Trial of Jesus,* trans. from 2d German ed. by Isabel and Florence McHugh (Westminster, Maryland: Newman, 1959), pp. 149-157—Trans.]

at the trial of Jesus. Thus the stipulation that trials could
be conducted only during the day may possibly have derived
from the more circumspect procedures of the Pharisees, who
were opposed to conducting night sessions lest a judge might
sometime grow weary and inadvertently render a wrong
verdict. The rule that a capital case could not be terminated
before the second day of the proceeding could also reflect
this desire to avoid a wrong verdict at all possible costs. In
addition, the narrower definition of blasphemy could only
have been introduced by the rabbis, who by virtue of restrict-
ing the crime to the matter of uttering the name of Yahweh
would not be obliged to start as many proceedings against
violators of the statute. Finally, one should probably not
stress unduly the question as to where the Sanhedrin conducted its proceeding against Jesus, especially since even the
evangelists do not clearly identify the place of meeting.

But if such considerations enable us to eliminate a major
portion of the contradictions between the Mishna and the
Gospels, how then are we to evaluate the relationship of the
Gospel accounts to the then current Jewish law? Blinzler
takes the position that the trial proceeding as described in
the Gospels is completely congruous with the Sadducean interpretation of the law, and that consequently no significant
discrepancy exists.[16] However correct he may have been in
pointing up the differences between the law of the Pharisees
and that of the Sadducees, Blinzler's position on this point is
untenable. By way of criticism it is necessary to state first of
all that very little is actually known about the specifics of
Sadducean law. Above all, however, there still remains a
serious contradiction, namely, that the commandment concerning the holy day was interpreted even more strictly in
the time of Jesus than it was later at the time of the
Mishna.[17]
It must therefore be viewed as quite impossible for the

[16] Blinzler, *Der Prozess Jesu, op. cit.*, p. 163; *The Trial of Jesus, op. cit.*,
p. 157.
[17] See Eduard Lohse, "Sabbaton," *Theologisches Wörterbuch zum Neuen
Testament, op. cit.*, VII, 9-10.

Sanhedrin to have proceeded on the Passover, or even on the Day of Preparation, to try a case in which a verdict involving life or death for the accused had to be rendered. This contradiction would still not be eliminated even if with respect to the sequence of the passion events one were to follow the Johannine rather than the Synoptic chronology and accept not the Passover itself but the Day of Preparation as the day when Jesus was tried before the Sanhedrin. For Days of Preparation were equally proscribed as days when trial proceedings could take place. Certainly a number of discrepancies between the Synoptic account and the stipulations of the Mishna can be resolved on the basis of the view that it was the law of the Sadducees which was in effect at the time of Jesus. One contradiction, however, remains. It is impossible to harmonize the account of the evangelists with the commandment concerning the holy day as found in the law.

The results of our investigation into the legal situation in the Palestine of Jesus' day thus compel us to return to the presentation of the Synoptic accounts and subject it once again to close scrutiny. Such an analysis can begin with the historically certain and attested fact that Jesus was executed not by stoning but by crucifixion. This means that it was a Roman verdict that was pronounced and carried out. Thus the governor did not simply ratify and allow the execution of a verdict which the Jewish authorities had placed before him for confirmation. For in such case, Jesus would have had to be stoned, as the law prescribed, rather than crucified. What then is the relationship of this historically assured fact to the account which the evangelists give of the proceeding before the Sanhedrin?

First of all it must be stated that the account in Mark 14:55-65 (cf. also Matt. 26:57-68; Luke 22:66-71) cannot be traced back to some eyewitness who at a later date might have told the Christians about the course of the proceeding. No disciple could have been present—Peter denied the Lord and the others had all fled—nor could any secret sympathizer of Jesus have been found among the members of the Sanhedrin who later on might have told the Christians what happened. There would be no point in thinking in this connection of Nicodemus (John 3:1-20) or of Joseph of Arimathea (Mark 15:43; Matt. 25:57; Luke 23:50; John 19:38), who in other contexts are spoken of as having been members of the council and who seem to have had some relationship to Jesus. For we simply do not know whether these men were present at the time. Since only twenty-three of the seventy councillors constituted a quorum, it is certainly possible that many members of the Sanhedrin were absent from this session. Yet in Mark 14:64 it is explicitly stated that "all" the councillors there present declared Jesus to be deserving of death. In other words, the evangelist does not give us the slightest reason to think that among the assembled members of the Sanhedrin there might have been even one who could be viewed as an informant, who might have passed on to the church a report of what transpired.

The evangelists' description of the proceeding against Jesus is not an integral unit but a composite of various parts. At the beginning there is placed into the mouths of the witnesses testifying against Jesus a strange word that he is alleged to have spoken: "I will destroy this temple that is made with hands, and in three days I will build another, not made with hands" (Mark 14:58). This word is found in the tradition not only here but also—in different formulations—at other points as well. Matthew follows Mark but omits the antithesis "made with hands—not made with hands" which suggests that the temple is set over against the new people of God. By this omission Matthew seems to be saying that the real concern here is with the rebuilding of the place of worship in the last days and that the continuity with the ancient people of God shall be preserved even in the consummation to come (Matt. 26:61). In the passion account of Mark and Matthew this word is once again alluded to, namely, when the crucified Jesus is derided by the Jews who stand about: "Aha! You who would destroy the temple and build it in three days!" (Mark 15:29; Matt.

27:40). In both places Luke omits the word about the temple; in Acts 6:14, however, he mentions that the charge against Stephen was that he was supposed to have said Jesus of Nazareth would destroy this place and would change the customs which Moses had delivered. This word about the temple is also cited in John's Gospel, though in connection with the episode of the cleansing of the temple which is thereby given special meaning.[18]

This word of Jesus about the temple thus appears within various contexts, and probably fits best in the story of the cleansing of the temple. Since it has been variously located in the tradition, it could hardly have been the real issue in the trial.[19] On the contrary, the evangelist seems to dismiss this first part of the trial by declaring the interrogation of the witnesses to be inconclusive inasmuch as their testimony did not agree (Mark 14:59). What is strange is that while Mark and Matthew tell us this statement was adduced by false witnesses, in the Fourth Gospel and Acts the very same words are attributed to Jesus himself, without any suggestion that they involved a false or groundless claim. The influence of the Scriptures is certainly evident here again in the mention of the malevolent witnesses. Psalm 27:12 says, "false witnesses have risen against me, and they breathe out violence." Just as in the Old Testament godless men rose up and testified against the righteous One, so now in the trial of Jesus false witnesses appear in order to deny the truth and slander the Servant of God.

After the testimony of the witnesses is broken off in this manner, the evangelist makes a completely new start and places the messianic question in the center of the proceeding as the decisive issue (Mark 14:60 ff.). The high priest stands up, walks over to Jesus and directs to him the question: "Are you the Christ, the Son of the Blessed?" (vs. 61). In keeping with the Jewish custom, there is here a reverent circumlocution for the name of God. What must strike us as strange,

18 See pp. 32-33 above.
19 For a divergent position on this point see George D. Kilpatrick, *The Trial of Jesus* (London: Oxford, 1953), pp. 10-13.

however, is that in this question the two titles denoting majesty—Christ (or Messiah) and Son of God—are placed side by side as if they were synonymous. After all, ancient Judaism never employed such a juxtaposition. Instead it scrupulously avoided the title "Son of God." To be sure, we read in the Old Testament the word God addresses to his anointed One: "You are my son, today I have begotten you" (Ps. 2:7). This passage, however, which ties in with the concept of the ancient oriental kingdom of God, is to be interpreted not in the sense of a divine procreation whereby a physical kind of divine sonship is established, but as a kind of adoption formula whereby the anointed One is invested with his sovereign rights and functions. Nevertheless, this passage remained rather isolated within the Old Testament writings. Neither was it used in post-biblical Judaism to introduce the term "Son of God" as a current messianic title. It is true that Psalm 2 was not forgotten; its phrases, as we know from Qumran texts, were in fact carefully remembered so as to keep alive the ideas connected with this messianically interpreted Psalm. Still, all talk about a divine sonship of the Messiah was avoided in order to preclude any possible confusion with the physical notion of divine sonship which was currently so widespread. This physical concept, which was known throughout the Graeco-Hellenistic world, could not possibly have been employed by Judaism as a designation for God's anointed One. It must therefore be regarded as impossible that the ruling high priest in Jerusalem should publicly have asked a messianic pretender whether he was the Messiah and Son of God. The linking together of these two titles in synonymous juxtaposition is thus to be understood as an act of the Christian church, for whom Jesus is not only the anointed One but also the Son of God. But this means then that the question placed into the mouth of the high priest marks the crux of the conflict between the Christian church and the synagogue. To the latter the Christian confession of Jesus as the Son of God must have appeared as a blasphemy it could not possibly tolerate.

Like the question of the high priest, the answer it receives is also formulated from the standpoint of the Christian confession. For Jesus does not merely respond to the question in the affirmative. He adds the words, "and you will see the Son of man sitting at the right hand of Power, and coming with the clouds of heaven" (Mark 14:62). In this verse the words of Daniel 7:13 and Psalm 110:1 are closely linked together, in keeping with the confession and the hope of the early churches, which not only believed in Jesus as the anointed One exalted to the right hand of God but also looked forward to his coming as the Son of man.

In response to Jesus' answer, the high priest—so the evangelist continues—tore his mantle and termed the assertion made by the accused to be blasphemy. In terms of the presuppositions of Jewish law, it is simply not clear what the blasphemy really was. Judaism never construed the claim of a messianic pretender as blasphemy. It did not even charge Bar Kokba with this accusation when he (132-135 A.D.) appeared as "son of the stars" and in vain fought for Israel's freedom, even though the failure of his undertaking proved that he could not have been the Messiah.

Although a claim to be the Messiah was not regarded as an offence against God's honor, the accusation of blasphemy leveled against Jesus is nonetheless perfectly comprehensible in the light of the conflict that existed between the Christian church and the synagogue. For it is a fact that the confession of Jesus as the Messiah and Son of God was the cause and subject of bitter disputes between the Jews and the Christians. The Gospel of John reflects this conflict when it tells us that the harshest accusation which the Jews could direct against Jesus is that he called himself the Son of God and thus equated himself with God (John 10:30; 5:17; 10:33).

If the concept of blasphemy has to be understood against the background of this situation, then the conclusion is inevitable that the Marcan description of Jesus' trial cannot be regarded as an historical report. It represents rather a formulation by the Christian church fashioned in connection with the church's confession and utilizing the proof from Scripture. Clearly identifiable are the references to passages already cited: Psalm 27:12 (in Mark 14:55-59), Isa. 53:7 (in vss. 60-61), Psalm 110:1, and Daniel 7:13 (in vs. 62). As the numerous references to the Old Testament show, it was impossible for the Christian church to relate the story of Jesus' suffering except in terms of its understanding of that suffering as a fulfillment of all that had been written and promised in the Scriptures. The church's main concern was to highlight this crucial aspect, and without regard to whether or not the details of its account squared with what was prescribed in Jewish law.

Behind the account of the passion story provided by the evangelists, however, it is nonetheless entirely possible to discern the historical sequence of the events themselves. Things probably took the following course. The Sanhedrin, whose Sadducee and Pharisee members were united in their enmity toward Jesus, had him arrested, gave him a brief hearing, and then delivered him over to the governor so he would be executed as politically suspect (cf. Mark 15:1; Matt. 27:1-2; Luke 23:1; John 18:28). It is no longer possible to determine the exact day on which this occurred. Just as it is impossible to answer positively the question whether Jesus' last meal with his disciples was or was not a Passover meal, so it is also impossible to ascertain with certainty the date of the arrest, sentencing, and execution. The earliest Christians were not interested in keeping and transmitting official minutes of these events. Their interest lay rather in speaking of the suffering and death of Jesus as the ground of our redemption and in accordingly proclaiming to Jews and Gentiles alike that Jesus was the Christ and Son of God. However the hearing before the high priest may actually have gone, it is certain that the Jewish authorities and the Roman procurator were ready to work together to bring Jesus to the cross. The Son of man was indeed delivered into the hands of men—those of both the Jewish authorities and the Roman governor (Mark 9:31; Matt. 17:22; Luke 9:44).

The Christian church had two objectives in mind when it recounted the proceeding before the Sanhedrin: on the one hand to stress the responsibility which the Jewish authorities actually bore for the condemnation of Jesus and on the other to emphasize that the confession of Jesus as the Christ and Son of God was the real stumbling block, an insurmountable offence to the Jews and incomprehensible to the Gentiles, both Greeks and Romans alike. The evangelist Mark, however, who took over the story of Jesus' trial before the Sanhedrin as it had been delivered to him by the church's tradition, gave special emphasis to the christological affirmations implicit in it. While in all the previous chapters of Mark's Gospel Jesus reveals himself only in secret as the Messiah and Son of God, here before the Sanhedrin he declares openly for the first and only time who he is, thus revealing the secret of his messiahship. For his messianic majesty and dignity can be understood properly only if it is viewed in inseparable connection with his humiliation, his suffering and death on the cross.

6.

The Crucifixion

In the hearing before the Roman governor the charge of blasphemy is no longer the point at issue. The accounts of all four evangelists agree that the question Pilate puts to Jesus is whether Jesus is the King of the Jews (Mark 15:2; Matt. 27:11; Luke 23:3; John 18:33). The question reveals clearly the accusation which lay back of it, which had prompted the Jewish authorities to deliver Jesus to the governor. Jesus is obviously stamped as politically suspect, a man whose preaching has stirred up intolerable unrest among the people. Indeed this is the pretext under which he has been delivered into the hands of the Romans along with the request that they dispose of him. In this connection the charge that Jesus claimed to be the King of the Jews could have been the result of a deliberate distortion of what he had been saying as he preached the lordship of God. For it seemed imperative to find some way of convincing the governor that Jesus had to be condemned and executed. At any rate, it was as a result of the representations of the Jews that Jesus was adjudged guilty of wanting to be King of the Jews (Mark 15:26; Matt. 27:37; Luke 23:38; John 19:19). The inscription over the cross carried this statement of the charge against him, and there is no reason to regard the formulation as a creation of the Christian church.[1] For the term King of the Jews or King of Israel was not employed by the early church as one of its christological titles. On the

[1] A divergent opinion on this point is expressed in Bultmann, *The History of the Synoptic Tradition, op. cit.,* p. 284.

contrary, it was the title of Messiah to which the Christian church gave new substance. It confessed its faith in the crucified One as God's anointed, and by holding that the messianic dignity of their Lord was grounded precisely in his death and resurrection the church in effect denied the claim which constituted the charge against him.

According to the Synoptists Jesus maintained silence in the face of the Jewish accusations leveled against him. He was mute like the suffering Servant of God. When in response to Pilate's question whether he is the King of the Jews Jesus answers affirmatively with the words, "You have said so" (Mark 15:2; Matt. 27:11; Luke 23:3), then this answer presupposes that the suffering Messiah, being completely resigned to God's will, could not possibly have pursued political ends. It is only the fourth evangelist who appends further explanations by having Jesus point out that his kingship is not of this world; if it were, the servants would have had to fight in their king's behalf, to keep him from being handed over to the Jews (John 18:36). The Synoptists confine themselves to a very brief account which merely mentions the charge leveled against Jesus and speaks of the impression which his majestic silence makes upon the governor.

For the early Christian churches—for whom the evangelists wrote their accounts—it was not necessary to identify Pilate. They knew from the earliest Christian proclamation that Jesus had made a good confession before him (I Tim. 6:13). Contemporary secular sources describe Pilate, who had become procurator in Judea in 26 A.D., as a harsh and ruthless man who performed the duties of his office viciously and avariciously, and who after ten years in office was finally deposed because he had precipitated a bloodbath among the Samaritans which led to charges being brought against him before the Roman legate in Syria. In the Gospels, however, the governor is pictured as one who performs the duties of his office, but who is also able to act contrary to conscience and better judgment when others bring pressure upon him. In such a portrayal there can be discerned the clear intention to assign a larger share of guilt to the Jews, and to exonerate the Roman governor as far as possible. It must have been important for Christians at that time that they be accepted as loyal citizens within the Roman Empire. This is why they were desirous on their part to establish a good relationship with the authorities, and not to reproach the Roman officials for giving heed—in the course of discharging their duties—to the accusations brought by the Jews against Jesus and the apostles and then passing sentence.

As in stories of the martyrs it is frequently recounted how the behavior of the innocent victim brings his judges and executioners to their senses, indeed often to the point of insight and conversion, so the evangelists here tell how astonished Pilate was by Jesus' majestic silence. Luke goes beyond Mark in having Pilate expressly declare at this point his belief in the innocence of Jesus (Luke 23:4). In an effort to extricate himself from the dilemma into which he has fallen because of the charges brought by the Jews, Pilate sends Jesus to Herod, who had jurisdiction over Galilee and who had also come to Jerusalem on the occasion of the Passover. As sovereign of the province from which Jesus came, Herod is supposed to take a stand (Luke 23:6-16). This amplification by Luke is unquestionably a legendary accretion to the original brief account of the hearing before the Roman governor. Martin Dibelius has convincingly demonstrated that the story of Jesus' appearance before Herod must have originated in considerations which resulted from a study of the Scriptures.[2] As it is stated in Psalm 2:2 that the kings of the earth set themselves and the rulers take counsel together against the Lord and his anointed, so now the Roman ruler and the Jewish king stand together as the judges before whom Jesus must appear while the raging mob demands his execution.

To be sure, the Roman governor—and all the Gospels agree in this—accedes only hesitantly to the demands with

[2] Martin Dibelius, "Herodes und Pilatus," *Zeitschrift für neutestamentliche Wissenschaft*, 16 (1915), 113-126; reprinted in *Botschaft und Geschichte*, (Tübingen, 1953), I, 278-292.

which the Jewish accusers confront him. At first Pilate
searches for some way whereby he might set Jesus free. We
are told that such a possibility presented itself in that every
year during the high holy days it was customary for the governor to release one prisoner on request of the populace. In
pursuing this custom it was Pilate's hope that the crowd
would ask for the release of Jesus. Instead of following his
lead, however, the people reject his suggestion three times.
In place of Jesus they ask for a certain Barabbas who was
imprisoned for murder and insurrection. Hesitantly and re-
luctantly Pilate finally yields to the wishes of the people, releases Barabbas and agrees to the scourging and crucifixion of
Jesus. Matthew emphasizes even more strongly than Mark
the great reluctance with which Pilate acceded to the will
of the Jews; in the end there was nothing else he could do.
A warning not to harm this righteous man comes to him from
his wife, who tells him of the dream she had had during the
night (Matt. 27:19). Pilate would like to heed this warning
but is practically compelled by the Jews to condemn Jesus.
In his helplessness Pilate washes his hands to protest his own
innocence, while the people willingly assume the guilt themselves, crying out, "His blood be on us and on our children!"
(Matt. 27:24-25).

The Barabbas story which is linked with the account of the
sentencing is again a legendary embellishment. For there is
no evidence anywhere of a custom whereby the people were
permitted annually upon the occasion of the high festival
to request of the governor the release of a prisoner. To be
sure, it occasionally happened throughout the Roman provinces that a governor heeded the people's intercession on
behalf of a prisoner and released him. But not a single docu-
ment mentions that such procedure had become a regular
practice.

It must also be pointed out that the picture which the
evangelists paint of Pilate is not in accord with the information derived from other contemporary reports. The non-
biblical accounts depict him as brutal and ruthless. The

evangelists on the contrary picture him as weak, submitting meekly to the will of the mob, unable to assert himself against the determined demands of the people who had been stirred up by the Sanhedrin. While the Marcan account tells us simply that in the end Pilate yielded to the Jewish accusers, according to Luke Pilate expressly attests that Jesus is politically innocuous (Luke 23:22) —thus indirectly of course attesting to the political loyalty of his disciples and of the churches as well. As we have already seen, Matthew underlines more strongly than the other two Synoptists the responsibility and culpability of the Jews in the death of Jesus. The fourth evangelist describes the face to face encounter between Jesus and Pilate as they discuss the problem of truth, and how Pilate is so strongly impressed by Jesus that he says to the crowds, "Here is a man!" (John 19:5). Only when the Jews warn that if he releases Jesus he is not Caesar's friend (John 19:12) does Pilate finally give in and surrender Jesus. Thus it is compulsion and pressure which forces Pilate to implement the will of the Jews and pass sentence on Jesus.

It is revealing to note how the picture of Pilate changed in the years following the formation of the New Testament. According to the apocryphal Gospel of Peter it was not Pilate but Herod who pronounced sentence on Jesus. Both the Jews and Herod refuse to wash their hands, thereby openly acknowledging their responsibility. But while Pilate washes his hands to testify that he is not guilty of this death, Herod gives the order to carry out the sentence. If the apocryphal Gospel thus exonerates the governor almost completely, Tertullian goes so far as to hold that Pilate was secretly a Christian.[3] A Christian legend even claims that he became a martyr, giving up his life at the end for Christ. The church of Ethiopia reveres Pilate as a saint. Thus the effort discernible already in the Gospels to absolve Pilate as much as possible of guilt in connection with the death of Jesus, and

3 See Tertullian, *Apology* xxi.

to assign sole responsibility to the Jews, continued in later years.

This undoubtedly represents a distortion of the historical facts. Although it is true that the Jewish authorities did press ahead with their plan to do away with Jesus, and for this reason turned him over to the Romans, it is likewise true that the governor did not hesitate long in complying with the demands of the Jews and having Jesus executed. Nothing that we otherwise know about Pilate suggests that he would have had any scruples whatever about having this man from Nazareth—who seemed so strange to him—nailed to a cross.

After the sentence has been pronounced and Jesus is led away, he is scourged and mocked before being taken to the place of execution. As the Roman legionnaires often played their cruel games with prisoners awaiting execution, so Jesus is now ridiculed as a pseudo-king. The evangelist Mark has set this second mockery over against the first in impressive contrast. Whereas Jesus was first abused as a pseudo-prophet and jeeringly challenged to utter a word of prophecy (Mark 14:65), here mock homage is paid to him in his royal garb in order to demean him even further (Mark 15:16-19).

In a few words we are told how Pilate's sentence is executed. They led Jesus out to the place of execution to crucify him (Mark 15:20b). During their stay in Jerusalem the Roman governors took up residence in the former royal palace of the Jewish rulers. They stationed a military detachment in the Fortress Antonia in order to command a direct view of the temple area.[4] The palace was located on the west side of the city and from here it was but a short distance to the place called Golgatha, which was outside the city walls in order that the crucifixion not be carried out within the city itself. The people who invariably gather upon such occasions to satisfy their curiosity could view the spectacle from the walls and from there hurl shouts of mockery and derision at the condemned person. At the place of execution a pole

[4] See Eduard Lohse, "Die Römischen Statthalter in Jerusalem," *Zeitschrift des Deutschen Palästina-Vereins*, 74 (1958), 69-78.

had been driven into the ground; to it was attached the crossbeam which the victim himself had to carry.

The scourging had made Jesus so weak that he was no longer able to carry his crossbeam to its destination. So a man by the name of Simon of Cyrene was compelled to carry it for him. Within the framework of the Synoptic chronology, which establishes the Passover as the day of execution, one would hardly expect to find someone coming in from the fields. For during the holy days the law of the sabbath was in effect, which prescribed complete cessation from all labor and even specified the number of steps a person was permitted to walk. The evangelist of course is not thinking here about the restrictions imposed by his chronological framework, and hence has no qualms at all about writing that Simon was on his way home from the fields.

The name of Simon of Cyrene is never mentioned again in the history of the primitive church. He was certainly not among the foremost members of the church in its early years. It is said only that he is the father of Alexander and Rufus. This reference to the sons—omitted by Matthew and Luke— may possibly have been intended to call the attention of the readers of Mark's Gospel to someone whom they knew. In the list of greetings at the end of Romans, a certain Rufus and his mother are named (Rom. 16:13), and it could well be that the reference is to the son of this same Simon. This mention of Simon serves no particular significance within the passion narrative. What it does is to provide on the periphery of the event the name of one eyewitness of Jesus' *via crucis*. This is in fact the only name we know of someone who was actually present.[5]

Upon arrival at the place of execution, Jesus declines the palliative of wine mixed with myrrh, and then is nailed to the cross. A few words merely state what happened (Mark 15:24a). In the succeeding verses several details are added

---

[5] See Martin Dibelius, "Das historische Problem der Leidensgeschichte," *Zeitschrift für neutestamentliche Wissenschaft*, 30 (1931), 197; reprinted in *Botschaft und Geschichte*, (Tübingen, 1953), I, 252-253.

which almost without exception describe the events of the crucifixion in language taken from the Scriptures. It was undoubtedly by ancient custom that the clothes and other sparse belongings of the victim rightfully became the property of the executioners. Usually they cast lots to determine which of them should receive each item. Instead of describing the procedure involved, the evangelist simply employs the words from Psalm 22:18, and without specifically identifying the quotation: "they divide my garments among them, and for my raiment they cast lots."

The brief account in Mark 15:20b-24a was written in the present tense; now the evangelist changes to the past tense in order to insert a time reference: "And it was the third hour, when they crucified him" (Mark 15:25). The titular inscription indicating the victim's specific offense is attached to the cross. To the right and left of Jesus two robbers are crucified, both presumably members of the zealot movement which sought by violence to end Roman domination and usher in the messianic age. Without specifically citing the scriptural passage, Mark certainly alludes to Isaiah 53:12: "he . . . was numbered with the transgressors." The verse is quoted directly in Luke 22:37, and in later manuscripts was inserted also into the context of the Marcan account (Mark 15:28).

The description of the mockery of Jesus as he hung upon the cross also follows closely Psalm 22. The righteous man of the Old Testament, forced to endure persecution and scorn, complains to God about his suffering: "I am . . . scorned by men, and despised by the people. All who see me mock at me, they make mouths at me, they wag their heads; 'He committed his cause to the Lord; let him deliver him, let him rescue him, for he delights in him!' " (Psalm 22:6-8). In these statements what befell Jesus had already been foretold. Those who passed by derided him. They wagged their heads and mocked him, jeeringly reminding him of what he had said about the temple (as quoted in Mark 14:58 in connection with the trial of Jesus) : if he is going to destroy the temple and rebuild it in three days, then let him at least manage to save himself and come down from the cross! (Mark 15:29-30). Enlarging upon this, Mark then adds that the chief priests and scribes also made fun of Jesus by repeating a challenge which the Pharisees had earlier hurled at him: let him now perform a miracle that will prove beyond any doubt that he is God's chosen One. If he is truly the Christ, let him prove it before the eyes of all by coming down from the cross (Mark 15:31-32). The evangelist tells us that the two men crucified with Jesus also joined in the mockery. Luke adds the legendary elaboration that one of the two criminals repented; in response to a plea that Jesus would remember him when he enters his kingdom, he received the promise that today he would be with Jesus in paradise (Luke 23:40-43).

The earliest tradition is short and to the point in describing not only the crucifixion but also the death of Jesus. From contemporary reports we know that the Jews whom the Romans nailed to the cross during the Jewish war sometimes lingered on for several days and that their lives gradually ebbed away in agony. Jesus had presumably been so weakened by the scourging and mockery that his death came after but a few hours. He uttered one last cry and expired (Mark 15:37). The death of Jesus too is viewed and interpreted in light of the Scriptures. His cry in the hour of death was a word from the Psalms, a prayer lifted to God by the suffering believer in the deepest agony of persecution and tribulation: "My God, my God, why hast thou fortaken me?" (Ps. 22:1; Mark 15:34). While this passage describes the bitterness of the suffering Jesus had to take upon himself, as a word of Scripture it also indicates that he yielded himself completely to the will of the Father, to whom he cries out as to his God, from whom alone an answer can come.[6] The cry of "Eloi" affords an opportunity to describe in greater detail the mockery with which the bystanders revile even the dying Jesus. They mistake "Eloi" for "Elijah" and scornfully ask

6 Cf. p. 10 above.

whether he has called upon Elijah to be his helper in need, to come with haste and save him (Mark 15:35-36; Matt. 27: 47-49). Luke places a different word from the Psalms into the mouth of Jesus: "Father, into thy hands I commit my spirit!" (Ps. 31:5; Luke 23:46), thereby bringing the bitter path of suffering to a conclusion that is replete with divine peace. According to John, Jesus dies with the majestic word on his lips: "It is finished" (John 19:30). He has accomplished the mission given him by God.

While Jesus' last hours are thus interpreted "in accordance with the Scriptures," Mark points up the significance of this death of the Christ by describing the signs that accompanied the end. First of all the evangelist establishes a precise chronological framework. Jesus uttered his last word from the cross at the ninth hour—about three o'clock in the afternoon. Already at the sixth hour a darkness had settled over the whole earth which continued until the ninth hour, the hour of Jesus' death (Mark 15:33; Matt. 27:45; Luke 23:44). It is impossible to find a basis for this statement in the proof from Scripture. Neither can it be viewed as a description of what actually transpired at the time. After all, the Passover was celebrated in the night of the full moon during the month of Nisan; consequently it was impossible for an eclipse of the sun to occur during the days of the Feast. We would also misunderstand the evangelist if we were to think that he intended to speak only of a darkness that was limited to the land of Palestine. He wanted rather to suggest that something extraordinary and inexplicable had happened. Concerning the events that were to precede the end of this world it had been said, "in those days, after that tribulation, the sun will be darkened, and the moon will not give its light, and the stars will be falling from heaven" (Mark 13:24-25; Matt. 24:29; Luke 21:25). Thus when it is written that a darkness settled over the whole earth, this is simply to indicate that in the hour of Jesus' death the whole cosmos was shrouded in darkness and that the end of this aeon had arrived.

The evangelist reports that a second sign occurred the

moment Jesus died: "the curtain of the temple was torn in two, from top to bottom" (Mark 15:38; Matt. 27:51; Luke 23:45). The question has been raised as to which curtain of the temple was here intended. For there was a curtain at the entrance to the temple which was visible to everyone. Some expositors, thinking the reference was to this curtain, have tried to interpret the statement to the effect that in the hour of Jesus' death it was possible to observe how his outer curtain was actually rent asunder.[7] However, in this instance—as in the case of the darkness just discussed—what is involved is again not the recording of a historical event but an effort at a theological interpretation of Jesus' death. The curtain intended, therefore, is undoubtedly that curtain which isolated the Holy of Holies and screened it from the eyes of persons who had no right to enter it. The transition from the old aeon to the new occurs in the death of Jesus. When the curtain which conceals the Holy of Holies is torn in two the way is now opened. By Christ's death we are all given access to the Holy Place. We may all now step up and draw near to God (cf. Heb. 9:3; 10:19-20).

Matthew goes beyond Mark in terms of the number of signs which occurred at the death of Jesus. He adds that "the earth shook, and the rocks were split; the tombs also were opened, and many bodies of the saints who had fallen asleep were raised, and coming out of the tombs after his resurrection they went into the holy city and appeared to many" (Matt. 27:51-53). The resurrection of the dead to take place at the end of time is symbolically anticipated in the resurrection of those who had been buried outside the walls of Jerusalem.

The Jews standing around the cross do not comprehend this meaning of what is here taking place. Only a pagan centurion surmises what has actually transpired and cries, "Truly this man was God's Son!" (Mark 15:39). The centurion thereby gives utterance to something which faith alone can confess: the crucified One is the Christ, the Son of God.

7 See Gustaf Dalman, *Die Worte Jesu* (2d ed.; Leipzig, 1930), I, 45.

Here too Mark was certainly not trying merely to report and describe. He wanted to have the centurion voice the faith of the Christian church, which alone is able to grasp the significance of what is happening.

Matthew and Luke have both changed the terminology of their Marcan source. Luke apparently asked himself whether it was conceivable that a pagan centurion standing at the cross could possibly have been able in that very instant to express his feelings in words of the Christian faith. Luke answered this question negatively and accordingly modified the verse in such a way that the words of the centurion now correspond more accurately to the actual situation: "Certainly this man was innocent!" (Luke 23:47). Thus the officer in charge testifies that the man nailed to the cross was an innocent and just man who should not have been killed. Matthew does not attempt to historicize like Luke. He is interested rather in refining the statement of faith. So he omits the word "man" altogether because it seems too mean and lowly to be commensurate with the unique majesty of Jesus. Jesus is Son and Lord. Therefore the words uttered by the centurion now become simply: "Truly this was the Son of God!" (Matt. 27:54).

To the words that Christ "died for our sins in accordance with the Scriptures," the earliest Christian proclamation adds that he was buried (I Cor. 15:3-4). The reference to the burial underscores the fact that Jesus pursued his path to the very end. He died as we die, and was buried as every deceased person is also buried. The Servant of God found his grave with the wicked (Isa. 53:9); thus even in the matter of his burial Scripture was fulfilled.

This brief statement of the Christian confession is vividly expanded in the Gospels by way of a detailed account. Since Jesus had died in the afternoon of the Day of Preparation, no time could be lost in arranging for the burial; it had to take place before the beginning of the sabbath at sundown. Joseph of Arimathea, a distinguished member of the council, who was also himself looking for the kingdom of God, went to Pilate and asked for the body of Jesus. Pilate registered surprise that Jesus should have died so quickly and asked the centurion to tell him whether Jesus was actually dead. Thereupon the request of Joseph of Arimathea was granted. He laid the body of Jesus in a tomb hewn out of the rock, and a stone was then rolled against the door of the tomb. In this story the Synoptists do not include even the slightest suggestion that, according to the chronological framework in which their entire passion narrative is set, it was still the day of the Passover and that it would have been difficult, to say the least, for anybody to have tried to buy linens and procure the other items required for the burial. This means that their description of the burial of Jesus is given quite without regard for the special rules demanded by the Passover observance, and likewise without any relationship to the framework which now encloses the entire account of the passion.

While all four evangelists name Joseph of Arimathea, John alone adds the name of Nicodemus, saying that he worked with Joseph in laying the body of Jesus to rest (John 19:38-40). It is entirely conceivable that a member of the Sanhedrin should have made it his concern to see that Jesus was laid in a grave, particularly since the law expressly stipulated that a hanged man "shall not remain all night upon the tree" (Deut. 21:23). The later tradition has enlarged upon the Marcan source. Matthew states that Joseph laid Jesus in his own tomb which was still new (Matt. 27:60). Luke emphasizes that no one had ever yet been laid there before (Luke 23:53), and John similarly reports that the tomb had never been used (John 19:41). It seems to have been their aim to show that a worthy place had been found in which to bury Jesus. Mark, however, seems not yet to have given much thought to this question. His narrative leaves us with the impression that Jesus was laid in the closest available grave and that a stone was rolled in front of the entrance to the tomb to block all access to the burial chamber and make it impossible for wild animals to break in. No special interest is shown in the grave itself. Its location is neither specified nor described. It is merely stated that Jesus was taken down from the cross and placed in a tomb. And it was not his disciples or relatives who bore him to the grave. It was the Jews, those same Jews who had taken him down from the cross (Acts 13:29). Thus is the reality of the death which Jesus died, plainly and bluntly described.

With the death and burial of God's anointed the passion story ends—but not the Christian confession! For the church which thus recounts Jesus' passion journey also confesses the crucified One as risen: "he was raised on the third day in accordance with the scriptures, and . . . he appeared to Cephas, then to the twelve" (I Cor. 15:4-5). It is because he was raised from the dead that his death has the power to atone—to blot out sins—and his suffering was for the forgiveness of sins (I Cor. 15:17). Having accepted this message and professed it in faith, the church now proclaims this event as the foundation of our salvation, because Christ died once —and therewith once-for-all—in order to win the victory over death. The Christian confession is bound to this specific historical event which transpired during the governorship of Pontius Pilate. This is why the church must necessarily give account of that event and pass on the story of what happened at that time.

In our examination of the passion narrative we have taken the presentation of the evangelist Mark as our starting point because he was the first to compose a written account of the suffering and death of Jesus. For the sake of comparison, we have from time to time called attention to the differences and peculiarities of the other Gospels. All four evangelists have in common the fact that they want the story of Jesus' passion to be understood in connection with the Christian faith and the preaching of the church and that their description of the passion therefore receives its stamp from the church's confession and preaching, in which it is the crucified Christ who is proclaimed.[8] The shape of the passion narrative has

8 See Bultmann, *The History of the Synoptic Tradition, op. cit.*, pp. 280 ff.

been determined above all by the constant reference to the
Old Testament. Although quotations from the prophets and
Psalms are frequently not specifically identified, words of
Scripture are nonetheless employed again and again to describe Jesus' path of suffering. Only the language of Scripture allows for appropriate expression of what really takes
place in the passion of Jesus, namely, that God's hidden
purpose, his promise and covenant, are here fulfilled and
that the crucified One is therefore God's anointed. The references to Scripture which are found all through the passion
narrative are an expression of the theological interpretation
of Jesus' suffering and death.

In addition to the proof from Scripture, however, other
motifs—discussed earlier in connection with particular passages—have also helped to shape the passion story. The worship activity of the church has found expression in the
pericope of the Lord's Supper (Mark 14:22-24; Matt. 26:26-
29; Luke 22:14-19). The paraenesis of the church can be
found in the words which Jesus addresses to the sleeping
disciples in Gethsemane when he summons them to watch
and pray (Mark 14:38). Apologetic considerations have
helped to shape the description of the trial before Pilate
(Mark 15:1-15; Matt. 27:11-26; Luke 23:1-25; John 18:28–
19:16). But finally and preeminently it was the confession
of the Christian church which played a significant role in
the formulation of the passion narrative. The same Jesus who
was humiliated, mocked, and beaten is the Christ, the
Messiah (Mark 14:61; 15:32; Matt. 26:63; 27:40; Luke
22:67-70; 23:37). He is the Son of man, who has been given
all power by God and who shows that power in suffering
(Mark 14:21, 41, 62; Matt. 26:24, 45, 65; Luke 22:22, 69),
who by his death redeems those who are his and gains a new
people drawn from all the nations of the world, and who will
come on the day of judgment.

The clearest expression of the church's confession of the
suffering and dying Christ is given by the evangelist Mark
at two points in the passion story. The first climax in his

presentation comes with the episode of Jesus' trial before the Sanhedrin in which the high priest asks Jesus if he is the Christ, the Son of the Blessed. The evangelist here stresses that Jesus' passion journey is understood aright only when this question is answered with the confession that Jesus is indeed the Messiah and Son of man. The evangelist brings us to the second climax in his account of the death of Jesus. Whereas the Jews heap only mockery and derision upon the crucified One, it is a Gentile who realizes that the humiliated One is the Son of God. The cosmic signs that accompany his death indicate that in Christ the decisive question is addressed to all the world. Everyone who ever hears or reads the passion story must face up to the question asked by the high priest: "Are you the Christ, the Son of the Blessed?"

Are we to say with the high priest and the synagogue that an affirmative answer to this question is blasphemy? Are we to despise and take offence at a Messiah who is crucified? Or do we agree with the pagan centurion who stood at the foot of the cross and cried, "Truly this man was the Son of God!" (Mark 15:39)?

Indexes

NAMES AND SUBJECTS

"Abba," 56 f.
Abel, blood of, 51
Active and passive voice, 5 f.
Acts, Book of, sermons in, 14 ff.
Adam, race of, 5
"After supper," 50
Aland, Kurt (ed.), 75 n. 5
Alexander, son of Simon of Cyrene, 95
"All" (many), 51
Altar, of the temple, 28, 30
Ananus, high priest, 77
Angel from heaven, 62
Angels, holy, 12
Animals, sacred, sacrificial, 23, 30
Annas, father-in-law of high priest, 74
Anointed One, God's, 7, 10, 13, 26, 42, 85 f., 90 f., 102 f.
Anointing of Jesus, 18, 21 f., 27, 65
Antioch in Pisidia, 16
Antithesis of flesh and spirit, 57, 59 f.
Antonia, Fortress, 94
Apocalyptic, Jewish, 12
Apocalyptic discourse, 33
Apocalyptic picture, 7
Apocalyptic sayings of Jesus, 21
Apologetic considerations, 103
Apostacy, 58
Apostles, 5, 14
Appearance of Risen Lord, 4 ff., 12, 102
Aramaic, 6, 51
Arrest and capture of Jesus, 14, 16 f., 19, 21, 61, 63 f., 66-70, 74 f., 87
Ascetic way of life, 47

Ass and colt, 23, 29
Atonement for sin, 52, 102 f.
Atoning death, 15, 18
Authorities, see Jewish authorities; Roman authorities
Authority,
    of Jesus to cleanse temple, 32 f.
    from the Lord, 36
    of scribes, famous, 36
    of Scripture, 9

Bar Kokba, 86
Barabbas, 16, 92
Barton, Dorothea M. (trans.), 12 n. 5
Believing in Jesus Christ, 1 f., 29
Bethany, 18, 22, 27
Bethphage, 22
Betrayal of Jesus, 18, 35 f., 40 ff., 61
Bible, 51
Billerbeck, Paul, 43 n. 7, 78 n. 10
Bitter herbs, 47 f.
Blasphemy, 79, 81, 85, 104
    charged against Jesus, 69, 79, 86, 89
Blinzler, Josef, 45 n. 9, 80 n. 15, 81 n. 16
Blood,
    of Abel, of prophets, and witnesses, 5
    of Christ, 51 ff., 92
    shedding of, 51
Body of Christ, 44, 49 f., 53, 101
Bornkamm, Günther, 50 n. 12, n. 13
Bread,
    dipping of, 40 f.
    leavened and unleavened, 37, 39, 47

and the Lord's Supper, 35, 48 ff.
and wine, 48, 53
Bultmann, Rudolf, 3 n. 1, 10 n. 4,
    40 n. 5, 89 n. 1, 102 n. 8
Burial of Jesus, 4 f., 10, 18 f., 44,
    100 f. (*see also* Grave of Jesus;
    Tomb of Jesus)
Buswell, Geoffrey (trans.), 28 n. 4

Caesarea, 76
Caiaphas, high priest, 74
Calendars, solar and lunar, 43
Calvary, 7
Capital cases, jurisdiction in, 74-78,
    81 f.
Captors of Jesus, 67 f. (*see also* Ar-
    rest and capture of Jesus)
Centurion, 99 ff., 104
Cephas, 4, 102
Charges against Jesus, 90 f.
Chief priests,
    scribes, and elders, 14, 33
    of the temple, 31
    and scribes, 11, 71, 97
Children, homage and praise from,
    28
Chosen One of God, 97
Christ, 53 (*see also* Jesus, Lord, the)
    appearance of, 4 f.
    belief in, 29
    buried, 4 f.
    church of, 39, 46, 49
    confession of, 29, 65
    death of, *see* Death of Jesus
    died for our sins, 4 f., 8, 15, 19,
        100
    encounter of, with Pilate, 93
    exalted, 2, 29 (*see also* Exalted
        Christ, Lord, One)
    friends of, 41
    message about, 9
    new people of, 103
    our Paschal Lamb, 46
    proclamation of Jesus as, 2, 13,
        69, 71, 87, 97, 103
    question ("Are you Christ?"), 71,
        84 f., 104
    raising, resurrection of, 4 ff., 14,
        90, 102 (*see also* Risen Christ,
        Lord, One)
    speech about, 2 f.
    as title, 85

witness about, 9
words of, 49 (*see also* Words of
    Jesus)
Christ-event, 2, 9
Christian, every, 41
Christian church, *see* Church, Chris-
    tian
Christian interpretation of Sermon
    on Mount, 13
Christian kerygma, earliest, 4, 9
Christian legend, 93
Christian message, 9
Christian understanding of Messiah,
    9
Christians, 8, 13, 25, 58, 61, 82 f.,
    91
    common task of all, 2, 61
    earliest, 2-5, 26, 48, 64, 87
        Palestinian, 41
    early, 9, 25, 35, 68
    first, 1, 17, 22
Christological affirmation of church's
    tradition, 88
Christological title, 89
Christology, earliest, 66
Church, the, 7, 13, 33, 35, 46, 50,
    52 f., 55 f., 83, 87, 90, 102 f.
    Christian, 6, 9, 11 f., 20, 26, 29,
        36, 41 f., 49, 54, 85-89, 100,
        103
        early, 63, 66, 89 f.
    confession of, 11, 65, 87, 102 f.
    early, 26
        in Jerusalem, 6
    of Ethiopia, 93
    faith of, 11, 39, 53, 100
    of Jesus Christ, 2, 28, 39, 46, 49,
        59
    of the Lord, 54
    paraenesis of, 63
    post-Easter, 29
Church, the,
    preaching and teaching of, 11 f.,
        102
    primitive, Palestinian, 5
        history of, 95
    proclamation of, 102
    tradition of, 88
    true, of Christ, 28
    witness of, 3
    worship of, *see* Worship of the
        church

Churches,
of all times and places, 61
Christian, 4
early, earliest, 1, 17, 52, 90
early, 86
Cleansing of temple by Jesus, 28-34, 67, 84
Clothes, see Garments
Colt, 23
Command of Jesus, 67
Communion with Jesus, the Lord, 48, 53
Condemnation of Jesus, 11, 16, 88 f., 92
Confession, 2, 104
of Christ, 29, 65
Christian, 85 f., 100, 102
early, earliest, 1, 6, 19, 51
of Christian church, 11, 13, 65, 87, 102 f.
of faith, 99
early, earliest Christian, 1, 6, 19, 51
Confession, of Jesus,
as Christ and Son of God, 9, 70, 88
before Pilate, 90
as risen and exalted Lord, 18
Confessions, 6
Congregation, 53
Conviction of Jesus, 71
Conzelmann, Hans, 28 n. 4
Corinth, 35
Corinthians, 4, 35, 49 f.
Cosmic signs, 98 f., 104
Cosmos, unbelieving, 31
Covenant, new, blood of, 51 f. (see also Old covenant)
Criminals, two, on cross, 7, 10, 96 f.
Cross, 2, 6 ff., 10, 33, 39, 87 ff., 94-97, 99-102, 104
inscription on, 89
journey to, 25, 29, 63, 65, 95
Crucified One, 10, 13, 27, 82, 90, 99, 102 ff.
Crucifixion, 7, 10 f., 14, 16 f., 21, 43 f., 48, 66, 82, 89-104
Cult,
Jewish, 67, 76
temple, 30 f.
Cultus of Old Testament Judaism, 46

Cup,
in the Lord's Supper, 48, 50
of suffering, 8, 34, 56
Customs delivered by Moses, 84

Dalman, Gustaf, 38 n. 4, 99 n. 7
Darkness at crucifixion, 98
David,
God of, 26
kingdom of, 24 ff.
second, 7
son of, 1, 24 ff.
Day of Preparation, 37 ff., 43 f., 79, 82, 100
Days of the flesh, Jesus', 64
Dead Sea, 6, 43
Dead Sea Scriptures, 58 (see also Qumran manuscripts)
Death, 7 f., 59
of Jesus, 1-4, 6, 9, 11-15, 17, 19, 29, 32 f., 44, 46, 51 ff., 69, 87 f., 90, 93, 97 ff., 101-104
time of, 21
vicarious, 53
Death sentences, see Capital cases
Declaration of Jesus Christ, 1
Delivery of Jesus to Gentiles, 11, 14, 61, 71 ff.
Denial of Jesus, see Peter, denial by, of Jesus
Dereliction of Jesus, 66
Devil, 58 f.
Dibelius, Martin, 3 n. 1, 10 n. 4, 14, 15 n. 6, 64 n. 6, 91 n. 2, 95 n. 5
Didache, 26 n. 2
Disciples, 11, 17 f., 20 f., 23, 28 ff., 35, 37-41, 47 f., 50, 53, 55 ff., 61 ff., 65, 67 f., 82, 102 f. (see also Twelve, the)
Discourse, controversial, of Jesus, 21
Disputes with the Jews, Jesus', 2, 31 f.
Divine law, 8, 61, 78 (see also Law, the, divine)
Divine sonship, 85
Doctrine, 6
Dodd, C. H., 15 n. 7
Dominical sayings, 65
Donkey, 23, 29
Doves, 30
Drunkard, Jesus as, 47

Ear, cutting off of, 67
Earthly sojourn of Jesus, 64
Earthquake at crucifixion, 99
Easter, 6, 11, 21, 29, 33, 53, 73
Eclipse, at crucifixion, 98
Egypt, Egyptians, 46 f.
Elders, 36
  and chief priests and scribes, 14,
    33
Elements in the Lord's Supper, 53
Elijah, "Eloi," 97 f.
End of time, 33
End of world, 98
Enmity to Jesus, 87
Enslin, Morton S. (trans.), 64 n. 6
Eschatological dealing (God's) with
  us, 59
Eschatological expectation of early
  Christians, 25
Eschatological thrust, 26
Eschatological transition from old to
  new, 46
Eschatology of Luke, 73
Ethiopia, church of, 93
Eucharistic words of Jesus, 18, 46
Eusebius, 26 n. 3
Evangelists, the, 10, 13, 20 f., 31 f.,
  36 f., 40 f., 54, 80-83, 87, 92 f.
  four, 4, 16 f., 46, 74, 89, 101 f.
Exalted Christ, Lord, One, 2, 6, 13,
  29, 33, 35
Execution of Jesus, 11, 14 f., 71, 74,
  82, 87, 89, 91, 94
  time of, 21, 95
Exegetes, exegesis, 35, 48, 59, 63
Exodus of Israel from Egypt, 37, 47

Faith, 6, 99
  call to, 15
  Christian, 100, 102
  of the church, 11, 39, 53, 100
  confession of, see Confession of
    faith
  in Crucified One, 90
  in Jesus as Messiah, 25 f.
  life of, 52
  losing, 55
  statement of, 100
  strengthening and confirming, 2
Fate, 20
Father,
  glorifying name of, 65

and king (God), 56
  will of, 97
  worship of, 31
"Father, save me," 65
"Feast, the," 34
Feast of Unleavened Bread, 21, 37 f.
Feasts of old covenant, 39
Fellowship,
  of friends of Christ, 41
  of Jesus with publicans and sin-
    ners, 53
  of the Lord with the church, 36
Fig tree, cursing of, 31, 29 f.
Flesh, sin of, 60
Flesh and spirit, antithesis of, 57,
  59 f.
Flock of Jesus, 53
Followers of Jesus, 2
Forgiveness of sins, 6, 8, 52 f., 102
Form of gospel narratives, 3
"Form-critical" investigation of gos-
  pel, 3
Formulas, formulation, 1, 4
Four evangelists, see Evangelists,
  four
Four Gospels, 4, 24, 74
Freedom, 59
Fruit of the vine, 54

Galilee, 16, 19 f., 76, 91
Garments,
  on ass's colt, 23
  casting lots for, 10, 96
Gentiles, 45, 76, 87 f., 104
  Jesus delivered to, 11, 14, 61,
    71 ff.
Gethsemane, 21, 55-68, 103
  tradition of 55 f., 61 ff., 66
Gift in the Lord's Supper, 50
Glorification of Jesus, 28 f., 65
Glorifying name of Father, 65
Glory, 8, 12
  of Father with holy angels, 12
  of God, 65
  kingdom of, 7
Glutton, Jesus as, 47
God, 2, 13, 45, 64, 96, 98 f.
  anointed One of, see Anointed
    One, God's
  armor of, 58
  Chosen One of, 97

combat troops of, 58
covenant of, 103
of David, 26
enemies of, 22
eschatological dealings of, with us, 59
as our father and king, 56 (*see also* Father)
gospel of, 1
help of, 60
history of, with Israel, 22, 58
honor of, 86
of Israel, 22, 58
Jesus calls on, 10, 56 f., 97
lordship of, 89
name of, 57, 84
nearness of, 53
people of, 45 f., 58, 63
plan of, 9, 20, 33 f.
pleasure of, 10
praise of, 28
promise of, 1, 103
prophets of, 1
purpose of, 103
right hand of, 73, 86
righteousness of, 8
Servant of, *see* Servant of God
supplication to, 57
spirit of, 59 f.
victory of, 60
will of, *see* Will of God
wisdom of, 34
worship of, 28
Godless, the, 7
Golgotha, 94
Good Friday, 6, 11 f., 21, 53
Good Samaritan, Parable of, 20
Gospel,
    form of, 1-4
    of God, of Jesus Christ, 1
    voice of, 2, 49
Gospels, 12, 19, 42, 75, 79 ff., 90 f., 100, 102
    Four, 4, 24, 74
    investigations of texts of, 3
    Synoptic, *see* Synoptic Gospels, Synoptists
    terminology of, 11
    writers of, 36
Governor, *see* Roman governor; Pilate, Pontius
Grace, 26

Graeco-Hellenistic world, 85
Grave, 8
    of Jesus, 9, 21, 101 f.
Greek, 5, 51, 59
Greek translation, 15
Greeks, 65, 88
Guilt, 8

Haenchen, Ernst, 15 n. 8
Halakah, Jewish, 79
Hall of hewn stone, 80
Hallel, Passover–, 42
Hallel Psalms, 24
Hasmonean princes, 76
Hauck, Friedrich, 63 n. 5
Healing,
    of lame and blind, 28
    of severed ear, 67
Heathen, 7
Heaven(s), 7, 24, 26, 73, 86
Hebrew, 6, 51
Hebrew manuscripts, 6
Hebrew text, 15
Hebrew way, ancient, 5
Hebrews, Letter to, 64 f.
Hegesippus, 26
Hellenistic milieu, 38
Hellenistic readers, 24
Heretics at Qumran, 45
Herod, 76, 91, 93
Herod Agrippa I, 77
High holy days (Jewish), 16, 24, 43, 76, 78, 92
High priest, 7, 69 ff., 73-76, 84-87, 104
    daughter of, 77
    palace of, 70, 74, 80
    servants of, 70
    slave of, 67
Hillelites, 42
Historical fact, 32
Historical Jesus, 2, 6, 12, 41
Holy city, 7, 16, 19
Holy days, 79, 82, 95 (*see also* High holy days)
Holy of holies, 99
Holy place, *see* Temple
    of Israel, 28
Holy week, 27
Holy Scriptures, *see* Scripture(s), holy
Homage to Christ, 18, 23, 25, 28

Hosanna, 23-27, 29
House of prayer for all nations, 31
Humiliation of Jesus, 1 f., 7, 25, 27, 29, 65, 88, 103 f. (*see also* Mockery of Jesus)
Hymn sung by Jesus and disciples, 42, 55

Incarnate One, 65
Innocence of Jesus, 91, 100
Inscription on cross, 89
Institution of the Lord's Supper, *see* Lord's Supper, Institution of; Words of institution of the Lord's Supper
Instruction, periods of, 2
Interpretation, words of (Passover), 47
Invitation to believe in Christ, 1
Israel, 7, 25
    freedom of, 86
    glory of, 7
    God of, 22, 58
    holy place of, 28
    king of, 24
    liberation of, 22
    lowliness of, 7
    redemption of (in Egypt), 46
Israelites, 47

Jairus' daughter, 62
James, 56, 62
    brother of the Lord, stoned, 77
    son of Zebedee, martyrdom of, 26, 77
Jar of water, man carrying, 38
Jaubert, Annie, 43 n. 8, 44, 45 n. 9
Jeremiah, 30
Jeremias, Joachim, 5 n. 2, 6, 7 n. 3, 17 n. 8, 40 n. 5, 45 n. 9, 46 n. 10
Jericho, 20
Jerusalem, 11, 13, 16 f., 20 ff., 38 ff., 43 ff., 48, 55, 65, 70, 72, 76 ff., 91, 94, 99
    destruction of, 80
    early church in, 6
    entry of Jesus into, 19-30, 39
    gates of, 2
    holy city of, 7, 16, 19
    Jesus' last days in, 3, 19, 31
    judgment against, 25, 28, 30

Jesus (*see also* Christ; Lord, the)
    activities of, 2 f., 29, 67
    anointing of, 18, 21 f., 27, 65
    apocalyptic sayings of, 21
    arrest of, *see* Arrest and capture of Jesus
    betrayal of, 18, 35 f., 40 ff., 61
    blasphemy, charged with, 69, 79, 86, 89
    burial of, *see* Burial of Jesus
    calls on God, 10, 56 f., 97
    church of, *see* Church of Jesus Christ
    cleansing of temple by, 28-34, 67, 84
    communion with, 48, 53
    condemnation of, 11, 16, 88 f., 92
    confession of, *see* Confession of Jesus
    controversial discourse of, 21
    controversies of, with scribes, etc., 33
    conviction of, 71
    days of the flesh of, 64
    death of, *see* Death of Jesus
    declaration of, 1
    delivered to Gentiles, 11, 14, 61, 71 ff.
    dialogue of, with Pilate, 17, 74, 89 f.
    disputes of, with Jews, 2, 31 f.
    as drunkard and glutton, 47
    execution of, *see* Execution of Jesus
    glorification of, 28 f., 65
    historical, 2, 6, 12, 41
    humiliation of, *see* Humiliation of Jesus
    innocence of, 91, 100
    as a Jew, 75
    as man of prayer, 65
    message about, 2, 4, 9, 39
    ministry of, public, 12, 16, 31
    passion of, *see* Passion of Jesus
    prayers of, *see* Prayers of Jesus
    prophecy of, 69
    raising of, 2, 4 ff., 11, 13
    rule of, sovereign, 33
    scourging of, *see* Scourging of Jesus
    sentencing of, *see* Sentencing of Jesus

silence of, before Pilate, 90 f.
surrender of, 41
teaching by, 12, 68
titles of, 12 f., 61, 85, 90
tomb of, *see* Tomb of Jesus
transfiguration of, 62
trial of, 14, 68-88, 103 f.
tribulation of, 64 ff.
warning of judgment by, 65
witnesses against, 69, 71, 83 f.
words of, *see* Words of Jesus
Jewish accusers of Jesus, 90, 92 f.
Jewish apocalyptic, 12
Jewish authorities, 17, 19, 21, 32 f.,
    66 ff., 76 f., 82, 87 ff., 94
Jewish Christians from Palestine, 38
Jewish communities, 7
Jewish cult, 67, 76
Jewish customs, 38, 84
Jewish expectations, 22
Jewish factions, 45
Jewish governing body, 76
Jewish Halakah, 79
Jewish hearers, 9
Jewish high holy days, *see* High holy
    days
Jewish king, 91
Jewish lands, 2
Jewish law, 77, 81, 86 f.
Jewish legal tradition, 80
Jewish objections, 9
Jewish origin of gospel, 12
Jewish people, 7
Jewish pilgrims, 25 (*see also* Pil-
    grims, Jewish Passover)
Jewish prayers, 56
Jewish rulers, 14, 94
Jewish scribes, 35
Jewish thinking, 59 f.
Jewish title (Son of man), 12
Jewish tradition, 61, 80
Jewish tribunal, 71
Jewish view, 61
Jewish war, 97
Jews, 5, 7 ff., 14, 16, 28, 30-33, 37,
    45, 67, 74 f., 77 ff., 83, 87 f.,
    90-94, 97, 99, 102, 104 (*see
    also* Jew)
    king of, 89 f.
Johannine chronology, 82
John the Baptist, 46
John the Evangelist,

Gospel of, 2, 16 ff., 24, 26-29,
    31 ff., 38, 43-46, 64-67, 74, 84,
    90, 93, 98, 101
    with Jesus in Gethsemane, 56, 62
    theology of, 74
Jonah, 56
Jordan Valley, 20
Joseph of Arimathea, 83, 100 f.
Josephus, 77 n. 9
Joshua, 36
Judah, 23
Judaism, 5, 12, 23 f., 26, 37, 56, 58,
    80, 85 f.
    Old Testament, 46
    pre-Christian, 8, 25
    post-biblical, 85
Judas 17, 34, 40, 55, 61, 66 f.
Judea, 20, 76, 78, 90
Judges, judgment, 7, 12 f., 22, 25,
    27, 42, 91
Judgment,
    day of, 103
    executed by God, 22
    against Jerusalem, 25, 28, 30
    of Jesus by Jewish authorities, 68
    warning of, Jesus', 65
Juster, Jean, 74 n. 4

Kerygma,
    concerning death and resurrection
        of Christ, 35
    earliest (Christian), 4, 9 f.
    of early church, 15
    of Good Friday and Easter, 12
Kidron Valley, 17, 27, 56, 66
Killing of Jesus, *see* Execution of
    Jesus
Kilpatrick, George D., 84 n. 19
King,
    God as father and, 56 f.
    of Israel, 24
    of the Jews, 89 f.
    messianic, 23 f.
Kingdom,
    of David, our father, 24 f.
    of glory, 7
    of God, 54, 85, 100
    of Israel, 89
    of the Jews, 89 f.
Kings of the earth, 91
Kingship of Christ, not of this world,
    89 f.

Kiss of Judas, 67
Kittel, Gerhard (ed.), 7 n. 3
Kuhn, Karl Georg, 45 n. 9, 58 n. 1, 62 n. 4

Last days, 7 f., 58, 60 ff., 83
  of Jesus, 3, 19, 21, 25, 31
Last meal (Last Supper), 18, 46, 48, 53, 55 (see also Lord's Supper)
Law, the, 8 f., 37, 59, 67, 79 f., 82, 101
  divine, 8, 61, 78
  giving of, 36
  Jewish, 77, 81, 86 f.
  of sabbath, 95
Lazarus, raising of, 22
Legal situation in Jesus' day, 82
Legal tradition, Jewish, 80
Legend, Christian, 93
Legendary elaboration, etc., 91 f., 97
Legendary motiv, 39
Letter, servitude to, 49
Levertoff, Paul P. (trans.), 38 n. 4
Liberation of righteous, 7
Lietzmann, Hans, 35 n. 1, 74, 75 n. 5
Life, 52
  of Jesus, 1, 12, 54
  sacrificed, 51
  in Jesus Christ, in his name, 2 f.
Lightfoot, R. H., 33 n. 6
Linens, burial, 101
Liturgical act, 51
Liturgical cast, 49
Liturgical cry, 26
Liturgical phrases, 50
Liturgical tradition of Judaism, 24
Liturgy, 47
  of the Lord's Supper, 26, 48
  Passover, 47
Logion,
  Jesus (destruction of temple), 32
  from paraenesis of early church, 63, 66
  "spirit is willing," 57
  entering into temptation, 58
Logos, 4
Lohse, Eduard, 24 n. 1, 28 n. 4, 47 n. 11, 71 n. 1, 75 n. 7, 81 n. 17, 94 n. 4

Lord, the, 23, 29, 91
  coming of, 26 f., 54
  confession of, 18
  denied, 70, 80 (see also Peter, denial by, of Jesus)
  despised and humiliated, 69
  exalted, 6, 13, 35
  fellowship of, with church, 36
  Jesus, reigns as, proclaimed as, 1 f., 7
  last meal of, 18 (see also Last meal)
  majesty of, 73
  name of, 24 f., 27 f.
  people of, 29, 52
  risen, 6, 63
  as truly present, 49
Lord's Supper, 17 f., 72, 103
  celebration of, 26, 35 f., 48, 50, 52 f.
  institution of, 17, 35-54
  words of, see Words of institution of the Lord's Supper
  liturgy of, 26
  tradition of, see Tradition of the Lord's Supper
Lots, cast for garments, 10, 96
Love, life of, 52
Lucan style, 15
Lucan tradition, 40
Luke,
  author of Acts, 15, 84
  eschatology of, 73
  evangelist, Gospel of, 11, 18, 27 f., 33, 38, 40, 45, 49-53, 62, 67, 70-74, 84, 91, 93, 95, 97 f., 100
  theology of, 73

Majesty, 8
  of Jesus, 100
  of the Lord, 73
Malchus, 67
Malefactors, two, see Criminals, two, on cross
Man,
  heart of, battlefield of, 60
  spirit of, 60 f.
Man to God relationship, 8
Manducatio impiorum, 53
Manual of Discipline, 60 n. 14, n. 15
Manuscripts, newly discovered, see Qumran manuscripts

Many (all), 51
Mark, evangelist, Gospel of, 1 ff., 11, 13, 17-22, 24 f., 27, 29, 33 f., 36-42, 45, 49 ff., 55 ff., 59 f., 62, 64, 67, 70-75, 83 f., 86, 88, 91 ff., 95-104
Marsh, John (trans.), 3 n. 1
Martha, 22
Martyrs, stories of, 91
Mary and Martha, 22
Matthew, evangelist, Gospel of, 11, 18, 23 ff., 27, 33, 40, 45, 49 f., 52, 67, 70 f., 83 f., 92 f., 95, 99 ff.
Matzoth, 47 f.
McHugh, Isabel and Florence (trans.), 80 n. 25
Men,
 fickleness of hearts of, Jesus knows, 55
 Jesus delivered to and killed by, 13
Message about Jesus, 2, 4, 9, 39
Messiah, 6 ff.
 Christian understanding of, 9
 claim to be, 86
 died for our sins, 8, 12
 Jesus confesses to be, revealed as, 70, 88, 103 f.
 rejected by Jews, 16, 20, 22 f., 25
 as ruler, 7
 suffering of, 7 f., 90
 title of, 85, 90
Messianic age, 96
Messianic dignity of Jesus, 73
Messianic expectation, 34
Messianic fulfillment, 61
Messianic interpretation, 23
Messianic king, 23 f.
Messianic meal of joy, 54
Messianic pretender, 85 f.
Messianic significance, 24
Ministry, public, of Jesus, 12, 16, 31
Miracle, 92
 of restoring temple, see Temple, destruction and raising of
Mishnah stories, 3
Mishnah, 80 ff.
 Aboth, 36 n. 2
 Sanhedrin, 77 n. 9, 79 n. 12, n. 13

Mob, raging, 91, 93
Mockery of Jesus, 10 f., 14, 69, 71 f., 94, 96 ff., 103 f.
Money changers, 30 f.
Moses, 7, 36, 73
 customs delivered by, 84
Mount of Olives, 17, 22, 42, 55 f.

Name,
 divine, 5 f.
 of the Father, glorifying, 65
 of God, 57, 84
 in Jesus', 2
 of the Lord, 24 f., 27 f.
Nazareth, 27, 29
New covenant, blood of, 51 ff.
New Testament, 6, 9, 53, 93
Nicodemus, 83, 101
Nisan, month of, 44, 98

Old covenant, feasts, sacrifices of, 39, 52
Old Testament, 5, 9, 14, 23 f., 39 f., 40, 56, 69, 73, 84 f., 87, 96, 103
 Judaism of, 46
 language of, 9 f., 23
 prophets, prophecies of, 28, 30
 quotations of, 15

Palestine, 6, 29, 38, 44, 75 f., 78, 82, 98
Palestinian Christians, 38, 41
Palestinian church, 5
Palm Sunday, 21
Parable,
 of barren fig tree, 30
 of Good Samaritan, 20
Paradise, thief in, 97
Paraenesis,
 earliest Christian, 57, 61
 of early church, 63, 66, 103
Parallelism, poetic, 23
Parousia, 12, 25 f., 29, 73
Paschal Lamb (Christ), 43, 46
Paschal lambs (Passover), sacrifice of, 37, 39, 43, 45 f., 51
Passion of Jesus, 3, 8, 11, 14, 16, 22, 25, 41, 54, 57, 73, 102 f.
 chronology of, 43 f., 82
 earliest account of, 1-19, 63, 66
 predictions of, 13, 20, 70, 72 f.

Passion journey, 4, 18 f., 102, 104
Passion story, 3 f., 10 f., 13 f., 16 f.,
    33, 37, 43 f., 48, 66, 87, 101 f.
Passive voice, 5 f.
Passover, Feast of, 20 f., 24, 37-40,
    42, 47, 79 f., 82, 91, 95, 98, 101
  chronology of, 43 f.
  lamb for, see Paschal lambs
  liturgy of (words of interpreta-
    tion), 47
  meal of (Lord's Supper as), 39 f.,
    42, 46 ff., 87
  pilgrims of, 22 (see also Pilgrims)
Passover-Hallel, 42
Paul, Apostle, 1, 4, 8, 17, 35 f., 46,
    48-53, 59 f.
  sermon of, at Antioch, 16
Pauline theology, 59
Pentecost, 15
People, 92 f.
  of Christ, new, 103
  of God, 45 f., 58, 63
  Jewish, 7
Pericopes,
  of cleansing of temple, 29, 32
  of delivery of the Son of man
    (Gethsemane), 66
  of entry of Jesus into Jerusalem,
    29
  of institution of the Lord's Sup-
    per, 18, 36, 38, 103
  of passion narrative, 72
  of preparation for Passover, 42
Perrin, Norman (trans.), 5 n. 2
Persian rule in Palestine, 76
Peter, 38, 62, 67
  apochryphal Gospel of, 93
  denial by, of Jesus, 55 ff., 70 f.,
    74, 82
  sermon of, 14 f.
Petrine tradition, 63
Pharisaism, 80
Pharisees, 7, 75, 80 f., 87, 97
  law of, 81
Pigeon sellers, 30
Pilate, Pontius (see also Roman
    governor; Roman procurator),
    14, 16 f., 71 f., 90-94, 100 ff.
  character of, 91 ff.
  dialogue of, with Jesus, 17, 74,
    89 f.

  as saint, 93
  wife of, 92
Pilgrims, Jewish Passover, 22, 24 f.,
    30, 39 f.
Porcius Festus, 77
Power,
  and glory, Son of man in, 12
  right hand of, Christ seated at, 26,
    73, 86
  Son of God in, 1
Praetorium, 74
Praise of God, 28
Prayer, house of (temple), 31
Prayers,
  of Jesus, 10, 56 f., 63 ff., 97
  thrice repeated, 61 f., 66
  Jewish, 56
Preaching, 1
  Christian, 8, 36, 41
  of the church, 11 f., 102
  of Jesus, 2, 67, 89
Preparation, Day of, 37 f., 43 f., 79,
    82, 100
Priesthood of temple, 30, 43, 45
Priests, elders, and scribes, 69 f., 76
    (see also Chief priests; High
    priest)
Proclaiming Jesus, 2, 7, 13, 87
Proclamation,
  cause of, 45
  of church, of crucified Christ, 102
  earliest Christian, 11, 13, 25 f.
  of Jesus as Christ, 2, 13, 69, 71,
    87, 97, 103
  of the Lord's death, 48
Promise of God, 1, 103
Promises of Old Testament prophets,
    73
Proof, scriptural, see Scriptures,
    proof from
Prophecy, prophecies, 28, 72 f.
  of Jesus, 69
Prophet(s), 1, 7, 13, 20, 30, 36, 72,
    103
  blood of, 51
  from Nazareth, 27, 29
  words of, 10, 52, 69, 73
Psalms, 41, 64, 73
  quotations from, 10, 56, 97 f., 103
Publicans and sinners, 53
Punishment, 42

Qumran, heretics at, 45
Qumran community, 43 ff., 58 f.
Qumran manuscripts, discovery of,
    6, 58, 60, 85

Rabbis, 49, 67, 80 f.
Raising of Jesus, 2, 4 ff., 11, 13
Ransom, 19
"Received and delivered," 35 f.
Redemption, 19, 87, 103
    of Israel in Egypt, 45 f.
Reeve, Dorothea H. G. (trans.), 35
    n. 1
Reformation tradition, theologians
    of, 53
Rehkopf, Friedrich, 40 n. 5
Remembrance of Christ's atoning
    death, 18
Repentance, call to, 15
Resurrection, 1, 6, 12-15, 32, 53
    of Christ, 90 (see also Risen
        Christ, Lord, One)
    of the dead, 99
Return of the Lord, 33
Richardson, Cyril C. (trans.), 26 n.
    2
Righteous, the 7, 12, 59
Righteous man, 96
Righteous One, 8, 84
Righteousness of God, by law, 8
Risen Christ, Lord, One, 5 f., 15,
    27 f., 102
Rising again, 70 f., 73
Robbers on cross, see Criminals, two,
    on cross
Roman, 76
Roman authorities, 91
Roman citizens, 78
Roman domination, 96
Roman Empire, 91
Roman governor (Pilate), 14, 16 f.,
    21, 66, 74 f., 87, 89 ff., 94
Roman governor(s), 76, 78 f., 91, 94
Roman legate in Syria, 90
Roman legionnaires, 94
Roman occupying powers, 29, 66,
    91
Roman procurator (Pilate), 87, 90
Roman provinces, 92
Roman road to Jesus, 22
Roman rule (of Rome), 75, 77 f.

Roman soldiers, 14, 66, 75
Roman state, 16
Roman suzerainty over Judea, 78
Roman verdict, 75, 82
Romans, 77 f., 88, 97
    Jesus delivered to, 89, 94
Rufus, son of Simon of Cyrene, 95
Rule, sovereign, of Jesus, 33

Sabbath, 21, 44, 79, 95, 100
Sacrifice,
    of Christ, the Paschal Lamb, 46
    temple cult of, 30 f.
Sacrifices at Mt. Sinai, 52
Sacrificial animals, 30 f., 51
Sadducean legal statutes, 80
Sadducean majority, 80, 87
Sadducees, laws of, 81 f.
Saints, bodies of, 99
Salvation, 6, 12, 52, 59, 65, 102
    age of, 32
    day of, 7
    history of, 45
    new order of, 52 f.
    way of, 8
Samaritans, blood bath among, 90
Samuel, 39
Sanhedrin, 14, 16, 21, 66, 69-72, 74-
    83, 87 f., 101, 104 (see also
        Mishnah, Sanhedrin)
Satan, 61
Saul, 39
Savior from heaven, 12
Schlatter, Adolf, 40 n. 5
Schmidt, Karl Ludwig, 3 n. 1
Schürmann, Heinz, 40 n. 5
Scourging of Jesus, 11, 14, 71 f., 92,
    94 f., 97, 103
Scribes, 11, 14, 33, 71, 97
    Jewish, 35 f.
Scripture(s), holy, 1, 4 ff., 8 ff., 14,
    69, 84, 91, 98, 100, 102 f.
    language of, 96
    in light of, 41, 56, 64, 97
    proof from, 10, 87, 98, 103
    words from, 66, 103
Self-examination, 41
Semitic character, 5, 41
Semitic expression, 6
Semitic original of Greek text, 6
Sentencing of Jesus, 14, 16 f., 66,
    69, 71, 74, 83, 93 f.

Septuagint, 15
Sermons, early (Acts), 14 f.
Servant of God, 9 f., 23, 25 f., 28, 33, 51, 68 f., 84, 90, 100
Sheep and oxen, 31
Sherwin-White, A. N., 78 n. 11
Signs, 2, 32
  at crucifixion, 98 f., 104
Silence of Jesus before Pilate, 90 f.
Simon of Cyrene, 95
Sin(s), 5-9
  atonement for, 102 f.
  Christ died for our, 4 f., 8, 15, 19, 100
  of the flesh, 60
  forgiveness of, 6, 8, 52 f., 102
  power of, 59
Sinai, 36, 52
Sinners (Gentiles), 61
Slave of high priest, 67
Soldiers, 17, 67, 75, 77 ff.
Son,
  of the Blessed, 69, 84, 104
  of David, 24 ff.
  of God, 1 f., 70 f.
    Jesus proclaimed as, 87 f., 99 f., 104
    title of, 85
  of man, 7, 11, 13 f., 19 f., 33, 41, 61, 66, 70-73, 86 f., 103 f.
    title of, 12 f., 61
Spirit, 57
  of Christ, 98
  of falsehood and truth, 60
  and flesh, see Flesh and spirit
  God-given, 59 f.
  of holiness, 1
  of man, 60 f.
Spitting on Christ, 11, 14, 70 ff.
Stephen,
  charges against, 84
  stoning of, 77
Stoning, 13, 77, 82
Strack, Hermann L., 43 n. 7, 78 n. 10
Streeter, Burnett, Hillman, 40 n. 5
Suffering,
  cup of, 8, 34, 56
  of Jesus, 1-4, 6-11, 16, 20, 23, 25, 27, 41, 63, 65, 67, 70, 75, 86 ff., 97, 102 f.

Surrender of Jesus, 41
Sword, the, 67
Synagogue, the, 9, 85, 104
  Great, 36
Synoptic chronology, 82, 95
Synoptic Gospels, Synoptists, 16 ff., 26, 29, 31 ff., 40, 42-45, 66 f., 70, 80, 82, 90, 93, 101
Synoptic tradition, 12
Syria, 90

Tabernacles, Feast of, 24
Table,
  eating at, 37, 39 f.
  of the Lord, 53
Table fellowship of Jesus, 53
Talmudic tradition, 78
Teaching,
  Christian, 36, 41
  of disciples by Jesus, 12
  in early church, 12
  of Jesus in temple, 68
Teaching of the Twelve Apostles, The, 26
Temple, 24, 27 f., 31 f., 39, 45, 68, 76
  altar of, 28, 30
  area of, 27, 30 f., 76, 80, 94
  cleansing of, 28-34, 67, 84
  cult of, 30 f.
  curtain of, torn, 99
  destruction of, 78
  destruction and raising of, predicted by Jesus, 32 f., 71, 83 f., 96 f.
  forecourt of, 30
  gates of, 27, 80
  of Jesus' body, 32
  priests of, 43, 45, 67
Temptation,
  of disciples, 58, 61
  of Jesus, 61, 65
Tertullian, 93 n. 3
Theologians of the Reformation tradition, 53
Theological affirmations, 45
Theological discussion, 75
Theological interpretation of Jesus' death, 99, 103
Theological statements, 39
Theology,
  of John, 74

of Luke, 73
of Paul, 59
Titles of Jesus, 12 f., 61, 85, 90
Time, end of, 33
Tödt, H. E., 12 n. 5
Tomb of Jesus, 101 f. (see also Grave of Jesus)
Tombs, opened, 99
Torah, 36
Tradition,
available to evangelists, 32
about Christ, 3
Christian, earliest, 14, 24, 46, 64 f., 71
of church, 42, 88
early, 15, 27, 97
fixed, 17
of Gethsemane, 55 f., 61 ff., 66
of hosanna, 26
Jewish, 61, 80
legal, 80
liturgical, of Judaism, 24
of the Lord's Supper, 17 f., 35 f., 38, 42 f., 46, 49, 51 f., 72
Lucan, 40
oral, 3, 17 f.
Petrine, 63
shaping of, 41
Synoptic, 12
Talmudic, 78
transmission of, 35 f.
of trial of Jesus, 70 f., 83 f.
written, 3
Traitor, identification of, 40-43, 52
Transfiguration of Jesus, 62
Transubstantiation, 53
Trial of Jesus, 14, 68-88, 103 f.
Tribulation of Jesus, 64 ff.
Truth (what is?), 17
Twelve, the, 4 f., 27, 55, 67, 102
Tyrian currency, 30

Unbelief, unbelievers, 33, 65
Unleavened Bread, Feast of, 21, 37 f.

Via crucis, 95
Via dolorosa, 3, 10, 33
Victory,
of Jesus Christ, 33, 65
over death, 102
Vine, fruit of, 54

Vinegar, drink of, 10

War Scroll (Qumran), 58
Warning of judgment, Jesus', 65
Washing of hands, 92
Watching and praying, 57 ff., 61, 103
Wegenast, K., 36 n. 3
Wicked, the, 8 f., 100
Wilckens, Ulrich, 15 n. 8
Will of God, 8, 10, 20, 56 f., 60 f., 64, 66, 90
Wine, 46 ff.
and myrrh, 95
Winter, Paul, 72 n. 3, 75 n. 6
Wisdom, 59
Witness,
to and about Christ, 9
of the church, 3
Witnesses,
blood of, 51
against Jesus, 69, 71, 83 f.
of trial, 82
of via crucis, 95
Woolf, Bertram Lee (trans.), 3 n. 1
Word(s),
of Christ, 49
of interpretation (Passover), 47
of Jesus, 3, 11 f., 32, 39, 55 f., 103
on cross, 10, 97 f.
eucharistic, 18, 46
on destruction and raising of temple, see Temple, destruction and raising of
of institution of the Lord's Supper, 35, 40, 42, 47-52
of prophecy, 72 f.
from Scripture, 66, 103
World, passing away, 26
Worship,
act of, 51
of the church, 18, 26, 35, 103
of God, 2
services of, 2
true, 28, 31
"Written, as it is," 5
Written accounts and tradition, 3

Yahweh, 79, 81

Zechariah, 28
Zimmerli, W. (trans.), 7 n. 3

SCRIPTURE REFERENCES

Genesis
49:11, p. 23

Exodus
24:3-8, p. 52

Deuteronomy
21:23, p. 101

I Samuel
10:2 ff., p. 39

Psalms
2, p. 85
2:2, p. 91
2:7, p. 85
22, p. 8, 96
22:1, p. 10, 97
22:6-8, p. 96
22:18, p. 10, 96
27:12, p. 84, 87
31, p. 8
31:5, p. 98
41:9, p. 41
42:5, 11, p. 56
43:5, p. 56
69, p. 8
69:21, p. 10
110:1, p. 69, 73, 86 f.
113-118, p. 24
114-118, p. 42
115-118, p. 42
118, p. 24, 28
118:25-26, p. 24 ff.
118:26, p. 24

Isaiah
50:6, p. 69
53, p. 51
53:4, p. 9
53:5, p. 9
53:7, p. 87
53:9, p. 9, 100
53:11, p. 9
53:11-12, p. 51
53:12, p. 9, 96
56:7, p. 31

Jeremiah
7:11, p. 30 f.
31:31 ff., p. 52

Daniel
7:13, p. 69, 73, 86 f.

Jonah
4:8, p. 56

Zechariah
9, p. 28
9:9, p. 23, 26
14:4-5, p. 22

Matthew
11:19, p. 47
16:21, p. 11, 70
17:22, p. 87
17:22-23, p. 11
20:17-19, p. 11
20:18-19, p. 70
21:3-7, p. 23
21:9, p. 24
21:9-15, p. 25
21:10-11, p. 27
21:12, p. 27
21:14-17, p. 28
21:23, p. 32
23:37, p. 13
23:39, p. 25
24:29, p. 98
25:57, p. 83
26:12-13, p. 18
26:18, p. 38 f.
26:19, p. 39
26:22, p. 41
26:24, p. 41, 103
26:26-28, p. 49
26:26-29, p. 103
26:28, p. 51 f.
26:29, p. 54
26:30, p. 42
26:41, p. 57
26:45, p. 103
26:47-50, p. 67
26:52, p. 67
26:57-68, p. 82
26:61, p. 83
26:63, p. 103
26:65, p. 103
27:1-2, p. 87
27:11, p. 89 f.
27:11-26, p. 103

27:19, p. 92
27:24-25, p. 92
27:34, p. 10
27:37, p. 89
27:40, p. 83 f., 103
27:45, p. 98
27:47-49, p. 98
27:47-50, p. 67
27:48, p. 10
27:51, p. 99
27:51-53, p. 99
27:54, p. 100
27:60, p. 101

Mark
1:1, p. 1
5:21-43, p. 70
5:37, p. 62
8:31, p. 11, 13 f., 20, 70
8:38, p. 12
9:2, p. 62
9:31, p. 11, 13, 20, 87
10:33-34, p. 11, 13 f., 16 f., 20, 70
10:45, p. 19
11-15, p. 3
11:1, p. 22
11:2-7, p. 39
11:3, p. 23
11:9, p. 24
11:9-10, p. 24
11:11, p. 27
11:12, p. 21
11:12-21, p. 29
11:17, p. 31
11:18, p. 31, 33
11:20, p. 21
11:27–12:40, p. 33
11:28, p. 32
13, p. 33
13:3, p. 62
13:24-25, p. 98
13:26, p. 12
14:1, p. 19, 21
14:2, p. 34
14:8-9, p. 18
14:10-11, p. 34
14:11 ff., p. 33

14:12, p. 37
14:13, p. 38
14:13-14, p. 38 f.
14:16, p. 39
14:18, p. 37
14:19, p. 41
14:20, p. 40
14:21, p. 41, 103
14:22, p. 36, 50
14:22-24, p. 49, 103
14:24, p. 51
14:25, p. 54
14:26, p. 42, 56
14:26-31, p. 55
14:32, p. 55
14:35, p. 56, 63
14:36, p. 56, 62 f.
14:38, p. 57, 59 f., 63, 103
14:39, p. 57
14:41, p. 57, 103
14:41b, p. 63
14:42, p. 61, 63
14:43-46, p. 67
14:47, p. 67
14:49, p. 68
14:50, p. 68
14:53, p. 69
14:53-54, p. 70
14:55, p. 69
14:55-59, p. 87
14:55-65, p. 82
14:58, p. 32 n. 5, 83, 96
14:59, p. 84
14:60-61, p. 87
14:60 ff., p. 84
14:61, p. 69, 84, 103
14:62, p. 73, 86 f., 103
14:64, p. 83
14:65, p. 70, 94
15:1, p. 21, 87
15:1-15, p. 103
15:2, p. 89 f.
15:16-19, p. 94
15:20b, p. 94
15:20b-24a, p. 96
15:23, p. 10
15:24, p. 10
15:24a, p. 95

15:25, p. 21, 96
15:26, p. 89
15:28, p. 96
15:29, p. 83
15:29-30, p. 97
15:31-32, p. 97
15:32, p. 103
15:33, p. 21, 98
15:34, p. 10, 21, 97
15:35-36, p. 98
15:36, p. 10
15:37, p. 97
15:38, p. 99
15:39, p. 99, 104
15:42, p. 21
15:43, p. 83

Luke
1:5-23, p. 28
7:34, p. 47
7:36-50, p. 18
9:22, p. 70
9:22, 44, p. 11
9:44, p. 87
12:8, p. 12
13:6-9, p. 30
13:33, p. 13, 20
13:34, p. 13
13:35, p. 25
18:31-33, p. 11, 70, 72 f.
19:38, p. 24
19:39-44, p. 28
19:45, p. 27
20:2, p. 32
21:25, p. 98
22:7-10, p. 28
22:8, p. 38
22:10-11, p. 38 f.
22:13, p. 39
22:14-19, p. 103
22:15-19, p. 49
22:18, p. 54
22:22, p. 41, 103
22:37, p. 96
22:40, p. 57
22:43-44, p. 62
22:47-48, p. 67
22:50, p. 67
22:51, p. 67
22:54-71, p. 70
22:66-71, p. 82

22:67, p. 71
22:67-70, p. 103
22:69, p. 73, 103
22:71, p. 72
23:1, p. 87
23:1-25, p. 103
23:3, p. 89 f.
23:4, p. 91
23:6-16, p. 91
23:22, p. 93
23:34, p. 10
23:36, p. 10
23:37, p. 103
23:38, p. 89
23:40-43, p. 97
23:44, p. 98
23:45, p. 99
23:46, p. 98
23:47, p. 100
23:50, p. 83
23:53, p. 101
23:54, p. 21
24:25-27, 44, p. 73
24:53, p. 28

John
2:15, p. 31
2:18, p. 32
2:19, p. 32
2:21, p. 32
3:1-20, p. 83
4:24, p. 31
5:17, p. 86
10:30, p. 86
10:33, p. 86
12, p. 65
12:1-9, p. 27
12:7-8, p. 18 f.
12:12-15, p. 26
12:13, p. 24
12:16, p. 29
12:20 ff., p. 65
12:27-28, p. 65
13, p. 43
13:18, p. 41
13:18-20, p. 40
18, p. 65
18:1, p. 56
18:1 ff., p. 17
18:1-11, p. 74
18:2 ff., p. 67

120

18:3, p. 66
18:10, p. 67
18:12-24, p. 74
18:25-27, p. 74
18:28, p. 43, 87
18:28 ff., p. 74
18:28 -19:16, p 103
18:31, p. 74, 79
18:33, p. 89
18:36, p. 90
19:5, p. 93
19:12, p. 93
19:14, p. 43
19:19, p. 89
19:24, p. 10
19:29, p. 10
19:30, p. 98
19:31, p. 21
19:36, p. 43
19:38, p. 83
19:38-40, p. 101
19:41, p. 101
20:31, p. 2

Acts
2:22 ff., p. 15 f.
2:23, p. 16
3:13-14, p. 16
5:30, p. 16
6:14, p. 84
7:54-8:3, p. 77
10:39, p. 16
12:2, p. 77
13:26 ff., p. 16
13:27-28, p. 16
13:28, p. 16
13:29, p. 102

Romans
1:1-4, p. 1
8:15, p. 57
16:13, p. 95

I Corinthians
5:7, p. 46
10:17, p. 51
11, p. 17, 46, 48
11:23, p. 17

11:23-26, p. 49
15, p. 15
15:3, p. 35
15:3-4, p. 100
15:3-5, p. 4 ff., 10 f., 14, 51
15:4-5, p. 102
15:17, p. 6, 102
16:22, p. 54

II Corinthians
5:21, p. 8
12:8, p. 57

Galatians
1:6-9, p. 1
4:6, p. 57

I Timothy
6:13, p. 90

Hebrews
5:7, p. 64
9:3, p. 99
10:19-20, p. 99

Type, 11 on 13 Baskerville
Display, Baskerville
Paper, White Warrens University Text